TRANSFORMING
THE MAINLINE CHURCH

TRANSFORMING THE MAINLINE CHURCH

Lessons in Change
from Pittsburgh's Cathedral of Hope

Robert A. Chesnut

Geneva Press
Louisville, Kentucky

Book design by Sharon Adams
Cover design and illustration by Rohani Design

First edition
Published by Geneva Press
Louisville, Kentucky

This book is printed on acid-free paper that meets the American National Standards Institute Z39.48 standard. ⊗

PRINTED IN THE UNITED STATES OF AMERICA

00 01 02 03 04 05 06 07 08 09 — 10 9 8 7 6 5 4 3 2 1

Library of Congress Cataloging-in-Publication Data
A catalog record for this book is available from the Library of Congress.
ISBN 0-664-50101-X

To my beloved wife, Jan

"Deep calls unto deep . . ." (Psalm 42:7)

Contents

Acknowledgments

For reasons that will soon become obvious, I have used no actual names for either church members or staff members in the book. Still, I must express my profound gratitude to all those present members of our ministry and program staff who have helped build our Cathedral of Hope vision into reality, some of them in a part-time capacity. In chronological order of service, they are Judy Menk, director of Christian education (1986 to present); the Rev. Hydie Houston, associate pastor (1990 to present); the Rev. Gail Ransom, pastoral associate for Taizé and the creative arts (1992 to present); Dr. Lois Lang, pastoral associate for senior and Stephen ministries and spiritual gifts (1994 to present); the Rev. Dr. Richard Szeremany, director of music and the arts (1994 to present); Patrice Searcy, director of the Family Enrichment Center, community and global mission and community development (1996 to present); Jeffry Johnson, associate director of music (1997 to present); Dr. Ellen McCormack, director of the Soul Center (1997 to present); Pam Kimmel, business administrator (1998 to present). I hold them all in high esteem and affection as friends and partners in ministry and thank them for their dedicated, faithful, and professionally outstanding service.

There are others who have served well—both past and present and mostly in part-time or interim capacities—and who have also made significant professional contributions: Jean Bray, Jan Chesnut, Marla Comedy, Patrick Ewing, the Rev. Dr. James Faltot, Dr. John Goldsmith, Dr. Joseph Willcox Jenkins, Gladys May, the Rev. Dr. Susan Nelson, Sam Pardue, John and Leslie Robinson, Ann Tucker, and Karen Vander Ploeg. Our office, facilities, and security staff—far too numerous to name—are the ones, often behind the scenes, who daily "pack our parachutes" for those of us on the ministry and program staff. Our indebtedness to them is immeasurable. My special thanks to Kim Carter and Norma Meyer, who provided invaluable technical assistance toward the end of this work when my own word processing skills proved inadequate.

I am grateful to our two pastors emeriti who have given me so much support by their frequent encouragement, kindnesses, and daily prayers for East Liberty Presbyterian Church and my ministry here: the Rev. Jack Myers (former pastor of Highland Presbyterian, which merged with East Liberty in 1981) and the Rev. Dr. Charles Robshaw, senior pastor, 1957–80. Dr. Robshaw's ministry, during especially challenging years in this community and congregation, provided visionary leadership for East Liberty's racial integration and its active involvement in community service and action. The Rev. Dr. Robert Hewitt, senior pastor, 1981–85, and the Rev. Dr. Gerald Johnson, interim senior pastor, 1986–88, continued this faithful tradition of pastoral leadership.

The lay leaders and members who should be thanked are innumerable. Some of them will recognize themselves in these pages. Not all of the good things all of them have done, however, could be included, for as John says at the end of his Gospel, "There are also many other things that [could be told]; if every one of them were written down, I suppose that the world itself could not contain the books . . ." (21:25). These Christian people know who they are, and to them I say with the apostle Paul, "I thank my God every time I remember you, constantly praying . . . for all of you, because of your sharing in the gospel . . ." (Phil. 1:3–5a).

Finally, my thanks to those who read all or portions of the draft manuscript of this book and offered me their helpful comments and suggestions. First of all is my editor, Tom Long, to whom I am indebted for all his encouragement, appreciation, and helpful suggestions regarding the manuscript. Other readers were Cynthia Chertos, Andrew Chesnut, Jan Chesnut, Jim Davidson, Carla Depperman, Bill Dodge, Lois Lang, Judy Menk, and Richard Szeremany. They bear no responsibility, of course, for whatever shortcomings may remain!

Introduction

Discovering Basement Treasure

In early December of 1992, I was searching for Christmas decorations in the basement of our Pittsburgh home. In the process I came across a college paper I had written thirty-five years earlier when I was a junior at the College of Wooster in Ohio. Submitted in the spring of 1958, it was an independent research project entitled "The Church in the Changing City: An Introductory Study with Emphasis on the Church in the Blighted Area."

As I reread this work, I was astonished by the continuing relevance of the conclusions that I had drawn so many years ago regarding what city churches must do to thrive and survive in a changing environment:

1. City churches drawing their membership from the city as a whole, as well as from their immediate neighborhoods, are in a unique position to reach all sorts and conditions of people, to become diverse and inclusive communities of faith.

2. Churches must be ready to meet the people of their area at the people's own level of need and understanding. This may mean, as an example, that churches of a more formal tradition of worship would be open to adopting more informal styles, including the use of gospel music, and so on.

3. Churches must extend their outreach through the mass media, advertising, and active promotion of their programs.

4. Churches should direct their mission programs to the needs of their immediate neighborhoods and work to solve basic community problems through community action and service, doing so in cooperation with other neighboring churches so that together their outreach to the local community is strengthened.

5. Churches must provide a seven-day-a-week program that is secular as well as religious, including education and recreational programs for all ages and both genders, day care for the children of working parents, and so on.

6. Churches should provide a community of caring and sharing for the lost and lonely, becoming inclusive communities that offer acceptance and affirmation of all people, communities that reassure individuals of their worth in the eyes of God, communities that provide values and standards on which individuals can build purposeful lives.

1

Just a few years after writing this paper, as a student at Harvard Divinity School, I had three years of wonderfully broadening experience with faculty and fellow students from an amazing array of religious persuasions. Our professors were Reformed and Presbyterian, Roman Catholic, Eastern Orthodox, Baptist, Unitarian, among others, and included world-renowned scholars such as Paul Tillich, James Luther Adams, Christopher Dawson, Georges Florovsky, Krister Stendahl, and on and on. Those years blessed me with a taste of the church universal and a lifelong vision of working toward a united church, truly catholic, truly evangelical, truly reformed.

What a marvelous, exciting time and place to be a theological student! These were the heady, early days of the young civil rights movement, of blossoming ecumenism, and of new visions for urban ministry inspired by the East Harlem Protestant Parish. It was in 1960, my second year at Harvard, that Presbyterian Stated Clerk Eugene Carson Blake and Bishop James Pike of the Episcopal Church made their proposal for the organic union of several mainline denominations, a proposal that I enthusiastically supported in an article for the Harvard Divinity School newsletter. (Now, it appears that this effort may finally bear some fruit by the year 2002, having spanned the entire length of my ordained ministry!)

During these early years, I also had two years of field experience in an urban church setting in downtown Boston. I learned in the process of running a storefront mission to unchurched people on the "back side" of Beacon Hill that my own theology of outreach was much more Tillichian than Barthian. Tillich's "method of correlation" called for meeting people where they are and offering the gospel in response to their existential situation, to the issues and dilemmas of their culture. This seemed to me both more Christlike and more effective than Karl Barth's approach. Barth's methodology denied any significant points of contact between revelation and reason or culture or psyche, thus denying any basis for a natural theology or philosophy of religion or apologetics. This struck me as leaving little option but to "throw" the gospel at people, much as one might throw a stone into a crowd.

The Harvard student who had preceded me in this storefront ministry was very much a Barthian. He had dubbed the place "The Parish of St. Ninian" (after a relatively obscure fourth-century missionary to the British isles) and offered little more than a formal liturgy that drew but a handful of Sunday morning worshipers. Once he had graduated, and I was in a position to make some changes, we rechristened our ministry "The Crossroads," gave the place a fresh coat of paint, and instituted a midweek evening discussion series called "The Crossroads Forum." Our topics included, among other things, the poetry of Ferlinghetti, contemporary religious art, existentialist theology, Protestant-Catholic dialogue, Massachusetts blue laws. Our guest presenters included the likes of Harvey Cox and Daniel Callahan, both still unknown Harvard graduate students at the time.

Ministry on the Urban Frontier

My first experience in pastoral ministry was as the minister of a new congregation in a blue-collar suburb of Cincinnati, where I was heavily involved in community issues and social action in the early days of the civil rights movement and the war on poverty. There in a small, loving congregation of people I would characterize as open-minded conservatives, I learned that it is possible for Christians with strongly differing views to live and minister together in mutual affection and respect. In 1966 I then returned to Harvard to start a Ph.D. program in Religion and Society.

While teaching courses at McCormick Theological Seminary in Chicago and directing the largely urban field education program in the mid-1970s, I discovered that my heart was still in the parish, and in 1975 I returned to congregational ministry, first in Norman, Oklahoma, and then in Evanston, Illinois.

However, it was not until 1988, when I became senior pastor of the East Liberty Presbyterian Church in Pittsburgh, that I had an opportunity to lead a truly urban congregation. Looking back now after a little over ten years in this position, I can see how absolutely essential were my basic learnings about urban ministry in that 1958 college paper. Those six insights reflected state-of-the-art thinking and practice in the field of urban ministry forty to fifty years ago and they are still fundamentally relevant today. These six points do need, of course, considerable amplification, elaboration, and practical application in the light of today's new realities—the task, in large part, of this book.

I would argue that these same six points, and others that I will add to them, have become increasingly urgent goals for the future of mainline churches everywhere, not just in urban areas. Urban churches have been on the frontiers of social change for many decades now. To the extent that they have survived by learning how to transform themselves, city churches have become pioneers, trailblazers for the church of the future. This is so because the same social forces that have long been at work in our cities are now increasingly setting the directions for change throughout our whole society. In race, ethnicity, national origin, and religious identity our society is becoming more and more pluralistic. It is in our cities that we find concentrated populations of young adults, racial and ethnic minorities, new immigrants, the poor, and sexual minorities. Issues of justice and equality are not going away. Neither are the challenges of our generational culture gaps.

When I was in divinity school, Gibson Winter's *The Suburban Captivity of the Churches* was much discussed in theological circles. Winter was writing in the thick of both the continuing post–World War II white flight to the suburbs and the emerging civil rights movement. He boldly named the problem for us—theologically, sociologically, and ethically—the problem that has only grown worse with each passing decade. Winter saw the increasingly racially and socially segregated character of the residential communities in which our churches were located and from which they drew their membership. He called it "the peculiar dilemma confronting Protestantism in the metropolis: How can an inclusive message be mediated through an exclusive group, when the principle of exclusiveness is social class [and racial] identity rather than a gift of faith which is open to all?"[1]

Consider: The Latino population of the United States, now 31 million strong and growing at a rate seven times that of the general population, is projected to become our largest minority by 2005. The white population of the United States, about 80 percent in 1990, is expected to drop to 71 percent by 2005 and to 53 percent by 2050. During that same period, the Asian population is expected to double in percentage, from 4 percent to 8 percent.[2]

Nor are the suburbs any longer escaping these demographic changes. The surburban population of the United States was 23 percent black in 1970, and the figure rose to 32 percent black by 1990. Some 40 percent of all minorities were suburbanites, according to 1990 census data.[3] All mainline churches are now challenged to face up to these social changes, to seriously reflect on what they mean for the ways we have traditionally "done church" and—if we want to survive and thrive—how we must begin to "redo church" now and in the future.

Mainline churches in our cities have, of course, been dying ever since the end of World War II. Consider: The number of urban Presbyterian churchgoers in Chicago and Philadelphia plummeted more than 50 percent between 1967 and 1997. The decline is even worse for Cleveland (over 65 percent) and San Francisco (more than 75 percent).[4] These figures would be even more disastrous if we made the comparisons beginning with 1947 or 1957.

Our urban church record is abysmal. Why? Could it be that, in most instances, we simply have not been putting into practice what students of urban churches have been advising for decades? In a word: Yes! This is the crux of the issue as I see it. While I am generally an optimist, in all honesty I must say that I have no false and easy hope that mainline churches have either the spirit or the will to do what needs to be done, even when the facts are staring us in the face. Although I believe this book charts the course we must take, it will also acknowledge just how difficult and painful the course ahead will be. But it is only when we have committed ourselves to that course and stuck with it that we may be entitled to any measure of realistic hope.

How We Must Change

Change is not easy. It requires sacrifice and courage, letting go of the comfortable and familiar and predictable for some higher purpose, some greater cause. Change is painful. Change will inevitably, of course, come upon us all whether we like it or not. The question is: Can we survive it, maybe even learn to welcome it and thrive on it as a gift from God?

Right up front, then, here is what is required of us in the mainline churches: Our focus must shift from providing worship and music and programming and pastoral priorities that are designed first and foremost to satisfy those of us who are already in the church. Our focus must shift toward reaching those outside whom we seek to draw inside. It must shift from the attitude that we are who we are now and will be so evermore, world without end. It must shift from the attitude that says, "If those outside the church want to change and become like us, fine; otherwise, they can go elsewhere, because this is who we are and this is what we have to offer."

Herein lies the heart of the matter: a fundamental spiritual challenge to clergy and lay leadership alike. Does the Christian faith inspire us to become open, generous, and generative enough that we can think first not of satisfying ourselves and meeting our own needs but reaching out to populations we have not been reaching—to the unchurched, secular, but spiritually hungry people (many of whom are our own children and grandchildren, brought up in our mainline congregations); to people of other races and cultures; to different classes and younger generations—in ways that will speak to them and meet their needs? A recent survey of Presbyterians does not give us a very encouraging answer. Fifty-six percent of the respondents said they believe that "most of their church members are comfortable with their church as it is and would not like to see changes in worship styles, music, or time of worship services."[5]

What This Book Aims to Offer

What I hope to offer in the pages that follow are some stories, some analysis, some practical suggestions, some promises and warnings, some biblical and theological reflection that will prod and inspire, encourage and guide churches to reach out in new ways, to rise to the challenges of change and growth that face us all in a new millennium.

Part I of this book traces the turnaround strategies and efforts in the first five years (1988–93) of my service as pastor of the East Liberty Presbyterian Church, a congregation that had already been in a steep membership decline for over thirty-five years. Part II continues the story through 1998, interweaving reports of ongoing innovations in urban ministry with accounts of the internal stresses, strains, and eventually the intense conflict with which our congregation struggled, especially in 1994–95. Part III addresses recent developments at East Liberty, then reexamines the continuing relevance of those six forty-year-old points for urban ministry on the way to exploring long-term trends and future projections for mainline churches.

Though the word "evangelism" seldom appears in these pages, I believe that this entire book can easily be read as a book about effective evangelism. *In fact, one of the most significant points illustrated in the pages that follow is how everything the church does—from education to music, from spiritual life to social service and action—can be and should be simultaneously approached as an opportunity for evangelism, for church growth.* This is a book about the kind of evangelism that Jesus practiced, an evangelism focused primarily on reaching those outside the faith community, those rejected and turned off by the traditional religious institutions. It is about an evangelism that is communicated as much in deeds as in words, especially in deeds of compassion, deliverance, healing, and social transformation, what we might call "incarnational evangelism." It is about a kind of evangelism that may well require more spiritual transformation of those of us within the church than it initially requires of those outside, those whom we should be trying to reach.

Some final words of caution here at the outset. First, please don't think, if your theological position happens to differ from mine, that there is nothing here for you. In fact, as you read, you will discover just how important to my own learning have been the insights of other Christians—both to the right and to the left—with whom I may have substantial theological differences. If we can maintain a spirit of respect for and openness toward one another, we can learn and grow in spite of our differences, or even because of them. Admittedly, for most of us this is easier said than done!

Also, don't be misled into thinking that smaller churches with fewer resources cannot learn from the experience of the Cathedral of Hope. Even with many resources, our congregation was in steep decline for close to four decades! Wealth and size are not the essential ingredients. The essential resources are spiritual and attitudinal. The essential gifts are those that the Presbyterian ordination vows ask of all elders, deacons, and ministers of Word and Sacrament: "Will you seek to serve the people with energy, intelligence, imagination, and love?" We must be clear, however, as Jesus himself was, that "the people" includes those outside the walls of our traditional religious institutions as well as those within.

PART I

New Beginnings:
Facing the Challenge of Change

So if anyone is in Christ, there is a new creation; everything old has passed away; see, everything has become new!

—2 Corinthians 5:17

1

Are You Ready
for Radical Change?

At First Sight

"Are you ready for radical change?" That was just about the first question I posed to the chairperson of the senior pastor search committee of Pittsburgh's East Liberty Presbyterian Church (ELPC). I could risk being frank from the outset, even outspoken, because I was a reluctant candidate. After more than eight years in Evanston, we were very much at home in the Chicago area and with our congregation. My wife, Jan, was happy with her work as head librarian at a Catholic girls' school and had begun work on a second master's degree in pastoral studies and spiritual companioning.

The Pittsburghers, however, were persistent. The phone calls and printed materials in the mail kept coming. Finally, in April 1988, I was persuaded to make a quick overnight trip to take a look for myself. I was astounded, profoundly impressed by what I found in Pittsburgh. The city itself was no longer the smoky, depressed iron city of legend, but a gleaming, bustling metropolis with beautiful hillside and waterway vistas to match San Francisco's. The city boasted strong cultural institutions—symphony, ballet, opera, the Carnegie Museums, to name a few—one of the lowest crime rates of major U.S. cities, extremely wealthy local philanthropic foundations that supported progressive causes and projects, healthy local neighborhoods with strong identities. In fact, in 1987 Rand McNally had identified Pittsburgh as the most livable city in the country.

The East Liberty Church, as I first spied it down Baum Boulevard from a mile away, was breathtaking. Outside of the great cathedrals of Europe, I had seen few Gothic churches anywhere to match this. The structure occupies an entire city block and the massive tower above it soars three hundred feet into the sky. The building had been constructed from 1931 to 1935, during the depth of the Depression, at a cost of $4 million. In that day, when many of Pittsburgh's most prominent families were members of the congregation, the building was a gift from East Liberty Church members Richard Beatty Mellon and his wife, Jennie King Mellon, heirs of the banking family's millions. The building was one of the last works of the illustrious Boston architect Ralph Adams Cram, who was also the architect for the first major stage of construction of the Cathedral of St. John the Divine in New York City.

Stepping into the sanctuary evoked another moment of awe—everywhere beautiful, towering stained glass of deep reds and rich blues from a wide array of America's best studios, carved stone and woodwork and Italian marble hand-crafted by European artisans, a majestic Aeolian-Skinner organ featuring 124 ranks and 7,743 pipes.

What really intrigued me, however, was what I learned from touring the rest of the church and visiting briefly with the church staff. This glorious, majestic structure was now housing nitty-gritty street ministries: a men's homeless shelter, a soup kitchen, a food pantry, after-school tutoring programs, and a summer in-the-city camp program for inner-city kids! Blacks and whites, urbanities and suburbanites, rich and poor were working and worshiping together here side by side. Twice a year, I was told, the church sponsored a community dinner at which church members and the neighborhood people served by these outreach ministries broke bread together.

Nevertheless, this was a dying church. For well over thirty years the membership, along with the East Liberty neighborhood, had been in steep decline. By 1989, the official membership was just one-fourth of what it had been at its peak in 1951, a drop from over 2,800 to a little more than 700.

East Liberty was once a thriving business and residential district. Up until World War II, the area surrounding the church was the third largest retail business district in Pennsylvania, exceeded only by downtown Pittsburgh five miles to the west and downtown Philadelphia at the opposite end of the state. Tall office buildings, major department stores, seven movie theaters, countless other shops and offices kept the streets and sidewalks of East Liberty bustling day and night.

Following World War II, however, as in many other U.S. cities, middle- and upper-middle-class whites started leaving the city for newer suburbs. Then a major but misguided urban renewal project, initiated in the late 1950s and completed in the early 1970s, proved to be a disaster for the East Liberty business district. A major street reconfiguration design sought to create a pedestrian mall at the center of the district, surrounding the church. With their customers unable to reach them due to the extensive construction work, many businesses died as the work went on and on.

In addition, the "renewal" plan included relocating a significant population of lower-income African Americans from their former homes in the Lower Hill District, near downtown Pittsburgh, into newly constructed, rent-subsidized high rises in East Liberty. The result, when it was all finished, was' that the newly created traffic circle functioned as a population moat, keeping whites outside, enclosing blacks inside the East Liberty core. Vacant storefronts and empty office buildings began to display the community's plight.

During my first visit, I was encouraged to learn that East Liberty Presbyterian Church had for some years been making conscientious efforts to respond to the new social and economic realities surrounding the church. In the late 1950s, the first black members joined the church. It helped that they were middle- and upper-middle-class, as were most of the African Americans who gradually followed them into the church over the next twenty-five years. By 1988, the congregation counted forty-nine black members, about 6 percent of the total. By that time the black membership had also become a bit more socioeconomically diverse and included a few single mothers on welfare.

Also during the 1960s, the church got involved with efforts of housing reha- bilitation in the community and gave leadership to the formation of the East End Cooperative Ministries, a coalition of Protestant, Catholic, and Jewish con- gregations united in a number of community service projects. East Liberty Church also provided leadership and financial support for the local community development corporation, East Liberty Development, Inc., which was working hard to undo the urban planning mistakes and promote economic growth.

In the early 1980s, East Liberty Church made space for twenty-four home- less men in one of the facility's small chapels that provided convenient street access. It was East End Cooperative Ministries that operated this homeless shel- ter plus the soup kitchen, food pantry, and tutoring programs that we housed rent free at the church. While housing some of these outreach ministries had ini- tially been the subject of considerable conflict within the church, it appeared by 1988 that these outreach programs had rather quickly come to be viewed by many members as essential ingredients of the church's new identity and mis- sion in its very changed neighborhood.

Still, the church kept on declining in membership. A manifold whammy of change was at work here. First of all, of course, mainline churches all over the country had been experiencing a continuous loss of members since the late 1960s. In addition, in its immediate neighborhood, East Liberty Church had been confronted with nearly four decades of population loss, serious economic decline, and major racial, ethnic, and cultural change. Obviously, the church had been changing with the community around it. But, also obviously, it was neither enough change nor the kind of change required to stem the unrelenting membership decline. Something more, something both urgent and radical was needed.

Thus my question to the chairperson of East Liberty's senior pastor search committee: "Are you ready for radical change?"

She paused and, then, replied, "We'll . . . change . . . anyway." She had point- edly dropped my adjective "radical." I would later learn, "radical change" meant for her something like introducing the passing of the peace into the Sunday worship service. For me, there was immediate clarity that the changes required would need to be both deep and wide, though I had only vague notions initially of many of the new directions needed, or of the many difficulties to be encountered on the path ahead. A few weeks later, I persuaded my wife, Jan, to return with me on my second visit to Pittsburgh. As we toured the homeless shelter and soup kitchen, she said: "This is what the church should be. This is what the church should do."

At the end of that weekend, as we said farewell to the search committee, a very bright and articulate member of the committee—and the only African American on the committee—put it to us directly. "On both of your two visits with us," she said, looking squarely at me, "you have quoted theologian Reinhold Niebuhr to the effect that the mission of the church is 'to comfort the afflicted and to afflict the comfortable.' That's good," she continued, "but I think maybe you should let that be applied to yourself. Maybe you are pretty comfortable where you are now in Evanston. Maybe you should consider if it's now your turn to be afflicted with us here in East Liberty."

To both Jan and me, that sounded like just about the clearest call that we had ever heard. It was also a far more prophetic message than we could ever have imagined at the time. It was true; we were comfortable where we were. In addition, we had in recent years often spoken with each other of the tug we were both feeling to be serving in a more racially and socially diverse context, somewhere that the church could be involved with just those sorts of community ministries that were already a profound part of life at East Liberty Presbyterian Church.

A Biblical Perspective on Change

When I was growing up, the popular assumption was that a person was pretty much a finished product by the time he or she had graduated from high school, or at least from college. After that it was just a matter of repeating the routines of adult life from day to day, year to year, performing the same fixed duties of work and family life, of church and community responsibilities. Continuing education, major changes of direction in adulthood, life as a dynamic process of continuing personal growth were strange or unknown concepts.

The accelerating pace of change in recent decades has forced a major change of attitude throughout our society. Most of us know that to survive in such a world we must not only adapt to change, we must even try to anticipate what's coming down the path ahead. Few things seem certain or dependable in marriage, family, work, or community life. We must keep on learning and growing throughout life. We must be flexible, adaptable, ready and willing to change.

Perhaps for some—maybe especially but certainly not exclusively for older generations—the world of organized, traditional religion is expected to offer a haven from the unrelenting pace of change in the world at large. In church at least, we should expect to sing the same hymns we sang in childhood, hear the same messages of an unchanging God from an unchanging scripture, follow the same absolute precepts and unchanging commandments, organize ourselves and do our ministry and mission the same way our congregations and denominations have always done these things. From this perspective, the Christian life is largely about standing pat, holding fast, keeping the faith as once delivered to our forebears.

Certainly there is support to be found in the Bible for this "stand fast in the faith" outlook. By and large, however, another perspective on change predominates in scripture. Beginning with Abraham and Sarah—called out from their familiar place to go they knew not where—people of faith in both Hebrew and Christian scriptures are portrayed as pilgrims, sojourners, even nomads. God is leading a pilgrim band on a journey that requires faith and risk taking in the face of much uncertainty about the next bend in the road ahead.

Both Jesus and the apostle Paul depict the life of faith as a process of growth, of development, of transformation. Paul speaks of the Christian life as a continuous growing up into the likeness of Christ. Toward the end of his life, imprisoned in Rome, probably facing a sentence of death, this remarkable pilgrim continues to write of the Christian life as a dynamic process of grasping the power of Christ's resurrection to grant the believer new life and growth:

> Not that I claim to have achieved all this, nor to have reached perfection already. But I keep going on, trying to grasp that purpose for which Christ grasped me. . . . I concentrate on this: I forget all that lies behind me and with hands outstretched to whatever lies ahead I go straight for the goal—my reward the honour of my high calling by God in Christ Jesus. (Phil. 3:12–14, PHILLIPS)

Metanonia—the Greek word for conversion—is prominent in the teachings of Jesus. It literally means to turn around, face the other way, and move in a new direction. The beginning of the Christian life is symbolized in baptism—a symbolic death, burial, and resurrection in union with Christ. The life of faith begins with a spiritual death of one's old self, old ways, old attitudes, old values. In faith, one is raised up with Christ to a new life, new ways and values and attitudes and priorities. In other words, from this perspective, the Christian life begins with radical change and continues with an ongoing process of personal transformation.

Those of us in the Reformed theological tradition are blessed to have a centuries-old watchword for our brand of Christian faith: "The Reformed Church, Always Reforming." Perhaps a better version for our time, however, and one clearly faithful to Jesus and the New Testament, would be "The Transforming Church, Always Transforming." And we should take this to mean, also in faithfulness to our tradition: transforming the individual believer, transforming the church, transforming the world around us.

2

Developing an
Entrepreneurial Church

Securing a Mandate for Change

East Liberty Presbyterian Church's search committee knew what they were getting. At least they should have known. I was up front with them from the start. I told them that I had no interest whatsoever in coming to preside over the death and burial of a church, that if I were to accept their offer it would be only with every intention of enabling a transformation, turning around the membership decline that had gone on for nearly four decades.

Like any other organism, many churches live an allotted number of years and then decline and die. Many die because they have outlived their purpose or cannot adapt to change. Some are ready to die. But not this one. Not East Liberty. If ever a church deserved to live and to thrive, it was this one—a unique church with a special mission and a wonderful story to tell to the larger Pittsburgh community. What was clearly needed was to start finding effective ways to get the word out about the good and exciting things going on here—the beginnings of an interracial, multicultural congregation, responding to clear-cut mission challenges right at its doorstep.

I told the search committee that the nation's leading church planner and consultant, Lyle Schaller, had written that any congregation really serious about membership growth should be devoting at least 5 percent of its annual budget to that cause. In this more urgent, even desperate situation, I suggested, it should probably be more like 10 percent. I knew that with an endowment of $18 million and an annual budget of over $1 million, they could well afford to do this.

I had a few fairly clear ideas about how to initiate a turnaround at East Liberty. At the church in Evanston we had enjoyed some good success by combining special events planning with major (for a church) advertising. We attracted new people by an annual Visitors Sunday with booths and displays and follow-up events designed to draw them back again. Rather bold, even controversial "image" ads in the local newspaper were helping the community get a new sense of an active, dynamic congregation that had long been regarded as a stuffy, stodgy, "country club" church. In fact, since the church was located close to the Westmoreland Country Club, some people even jocularly referred to it as "Westmoreland Presbyterian."

The East Liberty search committee also knew that I was not one to avoid controversy. The "trial sermon" I preached for them in what Presbyterians call the "neutral pulpit" of another Pittsburgh Presbyterian church focused on current issues of liberation theology and U.S.-supported repression and terrorism in Central America. Thus, I began my ministry at ELPC in September 1988, feeling that my intentions and my style were well understood and that I had been called to the church with a clear mandate for change. There was some initial resistance from fiscal conservatives, but we did succeed in getting the session to approve a 1989 budget that included an extra $75,000 for special events and advertising.

Jesus' Challenge to Become an Entrepreneurial Church

In his parable of the talents (Matt. 25:14–30), Jesus offers both a challenge and a promise, a warning and a vision. The parable also offers a model, a paradigm for the church that is at once biblical and secular, both ancient and modern. I believe it can be faithfully translated into our contemporary frame of experience as a model or paradigm for the church as an entrepreneurial enterprise, a new business start-up, a small-cap, high-risk, aggressive-growth venture. I realize that some readers may react to this as a crassly inappropriate paradigm for a Christian church. I can only ask you to bear with me through the following pages as we sort out exactly what it might mean to be an entrepreneurial church.

In this parable Jesus was speaking to the disciples he was leaving in charge after his departure, talking about what his followers were to do with the great treasure he was leaving in their care. First and foremost, the parable of the talents is about our stewardship of the gospel enterprise, our trusteeship of the good news of God's love and of the various resources with which we, the church of Jesus Christ, have been blessed.

What Jesus is saying to his church in this parable is, "Use it or lose it," "Risk and grow or wither and die." Jesus says the gift of God's love is given to us as good news that we must share in word and deed, even as he shared it. Jesus says we cannot clutch this gift to ourselves alone and bury it in a hole for safekeeping. It must be risked, invested, ventured with—all to the end that it is increased, multiplied, so that there will then be all the more of it to go around. The gospel is venture capital and if we don't venture with it, it will be taken from us. The parable of the talents says something even more challenging than

"Nothing ventured, nothing gained." It says, "Nothing ventured, everything lost!" Change and grow or wither and die.

Entrepreneurs, of course, are growth-oriented. So was Jesus. He was forever talking about growing things. For him the kingdom of God and the life of discipleship were not viewed as static places or things. No mighty fortresses existed in his image of the church. For Jesus the kingdom of God and the life of faith were essentially organic, dynamic, growth-oriented processes: little mustard seeds growing into great bushes, seeds planted in fertile soil, taking root, growing and bearing good fruit. The fertile soil for spiritual growth in Jesus' view was composed of a foundational trust in God that was expressed in commitment, courage, risk taking, a willingness to dare, to share, to venture, to innovate, to change and be changed. His entire ministry embodied these values and virtues.

Just Do It!

It seemed essential to move on the mandate for change at East Liberty just as quickly as possible. An appropriate sense of urgency about the church's decline could help overcome resistance to change. Some early successes would be good for morale and help to consolidate support for new directions.

In January of 1989 we brought in from my previous church in Evanston a bright, capable, thirty-something marketing professional who had helped us to formulate our marketing and advertising plan there. At East Liberty, she led a Saturday workshop on "Marketing the Church," open to any and all interested members of the congregation. Somewhat to my surprise and much to my delight, seventy church members participated, nearly 10 percent of the membership! It was an exciting, rewarding day of brainstorming and visioning, self-assessment and planning. What did our church have to offer? Who would be our natural "target market"? Where were the gaps in our ministry and programming when compared to the needs "out there"?

At the end of the day, we had a new advertising tag line for the church which also held promise as a mini mission statement: "Reaching Up, Reaching Out, Reaching You." The church newsletter was already called "Reaching Out." The rest seemed to follow, completing a threefold expression of our spiritual goals: reaching up to God in loving worship and devotion as the foundation of our life together; reaching out to one another and to neighbors near and far with Christian love and service; reaching out to the individual with respect and care for the uniqueness of each person.

Our "Marketing the Church" workshop also produced plans to follow through in the coming year with the development of a church logo, a new church brochure, street directional signs, a Visitors Sunday in September 1989, a follow-up special event in October, and an advertising campaign focused on the fall events. Moreover, as important as any of the above, we had laid a foundation of understanding and enthusiastic support for this new effort within a significant segment of the congregation.

In the fall of 1989, the church officers met to discuss a document entitled "Draft Intermediate Range Plan: A Document for Discussion." Following our first year of experience together, I had prepared this paper as a statement of my own reflections on the church's future directions. It contained my first use of the word "entrepreneurial" to define a strategy for the church and the utilization of its resources.

The plan was not comprehensive. A number of important dimensions of church life and program were already well in place. Christian education programming, for example, was in the hands of a solid committee and a very capable professional Christian education director. Already, under her leadership, the chancel steps at the 11:00 A.M. service were starting to fill with African American kids from the neighborhood, gathering there for the children's message along with the white kids who had been there before them. The Sunday church school classrooms were starting to fill again. A part-time youth worker had been hired and after-school drop-in programs for teenagers initiated.

Also, soon after my arrival, an early decision had been reached to replace the two interim associate pastors (both white, middle-aged males) with two permanent associates. That search process was well under way by early 1989 with an understanding that one associate would focus on membership growth and pastoral care; the other would help to lead our local and global mission efforts. We would also aim to make our professional staff more diverse in race and gender.

The intermediate range plan, then, focused on concerns of membership growth, stewardship, finance, and capital improvements. Following several hours of small-group and plenary discussion, our officers reached unanimous agreement to continue increased funding for special events and advertising for at least another three to four years; to set ourselves the goal of doubling the number of first-time visitors attracted to the church and doubling the percentage of visitors who became members; to update the church's antiquated electrical and lighting system; to install air-conditioning in the church offices; to increase the giving level of our congregation by seeking the help of a church fund-raising consultant in planning a special stewardship campaign.

By the fall of 1989 we had in place our new logo, a new church brochure, an advertising campaign, a plan for our first ever Visitors Sunday, and follow-up events. On Visitors Sunday a bagpipe and drum corps played a brief concert on the church's front steps, then piped us all into the sanctuary, down the center aisle, filling that immense space with the stirring reverberation of pipes and drums.

Our worship attendance at that service on that first Visitors Sunday was 523, more than double the average Sunday attendance for 1988 and considerably more than the attendance at any other single service for the entire year, including Christmas and Easter! With our lighting not yet improved, however, we knew we had more work ahead of us when a visiting child of about five was overheard anxiously asking his mother on that first Visitors Sunday as he cautiously peered into the dimly lit sanctuary, "Are there bats in there?"

Our follow-up events were also successful. In early November, a senior astronomer at the Adler Planetarium in Chicago flew into Pittsburgh to offer a well-advertised Saturday presentation on "New Visions of the Universe." With spectacular slides and films, the program traced the path leading from the big bang to the mystery of life on earth, inviting the participants to reflect on how this scientific view of our cosmic journey influences our conception of God. The next day our astronomer was in the pulpit at 11:00 A.M. worship. That afternoon our chancel choir and the choir of Trinity Episcopal Cathedral offered an inspiring presentation of Haydn's oratorio *The Creation*. In the course of these two days, a couple of hundred new people were introduced to East Liberty Presbyterian Church.

We ended 1989 having received forty new members that year, more than in any year for the past sixteen years. Our entrepreneurial efforts were well under way and beginning to bear fruit.

3

Would We
Rather Die Than Change?

One Tough Challenge

I should have known what I was getting into. Friends and colleagues across the country had cautioned me. East Liberty Presbyterian Church would be one tough challenge, possibly one of the very toughest in the entire denomination. The church and the neighborhood had suffered long decline and much demoralization. The previous senior pastor had stayed only four years, driven out amid conflict and vitriol. The congregational survey that the search committee had conducted as part of their initial self-study revealed that more than 60 percent agreed that "there are troublesome cliques in our congregation," and that nearly 70 percent thought that "a small group of people seem to make the most important decisions in our church." I also knew that the interim senior pastor had warned the elders that the subject matter of their meetings often focused on "rearranging the deck chairs on the *Titanic*." Accepting this call would mean trying to do a U-turn quickly with a massive and endangered ship!

It took me several years to piece the whole picture together, but eventually the basic dynamics became clear. Some factors here were endemic in other mainline churches that I had experienced elsewhere over the years. Other elements were peculiar to ELPC with its unique history and identity. Chief among its dynamics was the sad fact that the church had been, for many years, not so much a unified family of faith as a somewhat contentious confederation of factions.

One might even be tempted to speak of "turfdoms." In one sector after another of congregational life there was a small group of individuals—in some instances, just one individual—who had, many years ago, assumed control of that particular spot and then held on for dear life. Most pastors recognize this phenomenon: a men's or women's organization, an adult class, an ushering team, one committee or another (especially, it seems, those having to do with property and finance), a church treasurer, or a clerk of session. One church I served had the same clerk for sixty years! In another, one of our church organizations had a "president for life" who was also one of the leading opponents of bringing new people into leadership roles "too soon," before they had "proven themselves." In this case and most others like it, there are no annual elections, no rotation of leadership, just the same person or persons holding on to the same positions indefinitely. If and when there is any change of leadership in these positions, it is generally accomplished in a self-perpetuating fashion with outgoing leaders choosing incoming leaders.

I discovered that such turfs were more prevalent and persistent at East Liberty than I had experienced anywhere else in my twenty-five years of ministry. This probably has had something to do with the history of wealth, social power, and prestige that characterized the congregation in the past. Enough of that old aura lingered on in the collective memory of church and community that it continued to tempt some to claim their own little piece of what was still known in some circles as Pittsburgh's "Mellon Church." There were many tails here, each trying at various times and in various ways to wag the church dog.

A sort of musical chairs approach to board membership had also long prevailed at this church. The Presbyterian *Book of Order* limits board terms, but this was flouted by rotating individuals back and forth from the trustees to the session and back again. After a few longtime leaders began to object that our nominating committee was, under my influence, putting too many new people on the church boards who had not been around long enough to "prove themselves," I decided to do a little research. I found that there were thirty-five individuals in the congregation who had served on one church board or another for at least fifteen years—many of them for twenty, thirty, and, in one case, for fifty-five years!

Shortly before I arrived at East Liberty, the size of the session, the church's governing board, had been reduced because lay leaders had concluded that there simply were not enough potential leaders to fill the spots. This way of thinking had become a self-fulfilling prophecy as the same individuals kept on nominating and renominating themselves and their friends to office.

East Liberty was one of those congregations in which the board of trustees had long been unofficially viewed as the real "power board" of the church, even though, according to Presbyterian polity, final decision-making authority resides with the session. In my own experience, churches in which a board of trustees sets the tone and direction for the church often fail to display an entrepreneurial spirit. This is somewhat ironic since trustees are generally supposed to be leaders in the world of business and finance. But the fiscally conservative types who often wind up on church boards of trustees tend to be inherently risk-averse, uncomfortable with innovation. I have long suspected that the banker Potter in the movie classic *It's a Wonderful Life* was a trustee in the local Presbyterian church.

Where this "typical trustee" mind-set prevails—and it can certainly prevail in churches without a separate board—the focus is on maintenance rather than mission, conservation rather than vision. Church resources are, above all, to be preserved. Church endowments tend to become ends in themselves, left to accumulate into ever larger piles of untapped wealth. The building is to be kept under lock and key, rowdy neighborhood youngsters excluded, street people carefully watched and confined to only those parts of the building, if any, that are dedicated to community service. Building maintenance is accorded a far higher budget priority than mission and service programs and projects. The focus is inward, not outward. The lesson of the parable of the talents is lost, turned on its head.

A biblically faithful entrepreneurial church will be focused outside itself, reaching out to serve and to include those outside its walls, willing to change and innovate in order to accomplish its mission more effectively, developing its ministry and mission with the needs in mind of those it is trying to reach. The opposite model is a closed-corporation church, a monopoly, a private club, a self-serving organization with a self-perpetuating leadership that circles the wagons to outsiders and concentrates on serving itself and pleasing the insiders.

I learned long ago that not all church leaders welcome the growth of their church. They may give it lip service, but their hearts are not in it. First of all, churches that want to grow must be willing to change, sometimes to make fundamental changes in order to reach new people. However, if you are basically satisfied with things as they are and with your place in the scheme of things, why would you want to make such changes? Secondly, growth itself will bring change. New people with new ideas will upset the status quo. The real attitude that often prevails, therefore, is that if the newcomer can "fit in" to our way of doing things, fine. Otherwise, let them look elsewhere. More than once I have heard this viewpoint openly articulated by those willing to say honestly what many others only think.

Now, of course, not all trustees fit this mold. Not all longtime church members and leaders are dug in, committed, above all else, to defending their own power base. Many, in my experience, are truly committed to selfless service. In fact, without forward-looking trustees and visionary longtime members and leaders who were willing to break the molds of tradition, no significant change could have been accomplished at East Liberty Presbyterian Church.

I will always be grateful to one lifetime member and longtime church officer who was president of the board of trustees in my first year and a half at East Liberty. The openness, the intelligence, the ability, the selfless dedication to the well-being of the church, the willingness to endorse change and to envision a new future for the congregation, the genuine care and concern for our inner-city neighborhood and its people demonstrated by this outstanding Christian and his wife were absolutely essential to our successes in the early years. He got us through what would have been an otherwise tough start with an otherwise difficult board of trustees. Later he chaired our strategic planning committee. His wife moved us forward with our growth agenda during four exciting and fruitful early years when she served as the extraordinarily able and visionary chairperson of our membership and growth committee. Later, at a critical juncture, she chaired our nominating committee and assured that the process got opened up to new people. And these two are by no means alone. There were and are many other longtime East Liberty members and officers with incredibly good hearts and open minds, ready to change and to be changed.

Getting Stuck in 1955

The challenges we have faced at East Liberty may be, in some respects, unique or relatively extreme, but many of them are also typical of thousands of mainline churches all across the country. A few years ago I was teaching a course on "Urban Church Growth/Evangelism" at Pittsburgh Theological Seminary. The brightest and best student in the class was a young Presbyterian pastor who had been laboring for nine years in a challenging church redevelopment situation. He had experienced some good success, but it had been slow going and often discouraging. It was especially dismaying to hear his account of his failure at trying to start a new alternative service on Saturday evening. It was not that the service itself was a failure. Far from it. The new service quickly began to draw a significant number of new people to the church. But the service was eventually canceled because the new people and the new style of worship were just too threatening to some of the influential, longtime members of that church.

About the same time I was hearing of this young pastor's frustrating struggle to facilitate change and renewal, I learned of another sad development between two Presbyterian congregations in a nearby city. Over the past couple of decades, the population there had shifted decidedly from a white to a black majority. Once there were six Presbyterian churches in that community; now two were left. Each congregation had concluded that separately they had just a few years left to live, so the two decided to study the possibility of merging with each other. However, once they looked squarely at the changes that would be required in their schedules, their meeting place, their programming and governance, they decided to go their separate ways and die.

At the same time, the building of one of the defunct Presbyterian churches in that town was being filled to overflowing by a new, rapidly growing, nondenominational congregation that was bringing together an exciting mix of blacks and whites, poor and middle class in worship experiences offering a rich variety of musical cultures. That congregation was also reaching out in many vital ways to serve the needs of its community.

Many of our mainline churches all over the country are dominated by longtime, locked-in leadership elites that really would rather see their churches die than change. Thickets of self-satisfaction, complacency, and exclusivity have overgrown and choked out any sprouts of entrepreneurial spirit while we have kept on trying to live in the afterglow of glory days long gone. One definition of insanity, it has been suggested, is continuing to do the same old things the old way, over and over again, yet expecting different results.

In 1995 one local church organization I know kept turning out documents that read "1955" rather than the correct date. It was a revealing error. The leaders of that organization were in their young adult prime in 1955, just as East Liberty and many of our mainline churches were in their prime during the same era. In 1995 these folks were still living in 1955 and doing things in their organization pretty much as they had learned to do them forty years before.

Staying stuck in 1955 (or '65 or '75 or '85 or '95) won't work for our churches any better than it worked for the Detroit automakers. Analysts have said that one of the big problems in Detroit until fairly recently was that auto executives kept on making the kind of cars that they themselves liked and enjoyed driving to the office from their suburban homes, even after it became clear that a majority of the American public wanted something else. We're doing exactly the same thing in our churches when we plan our worship and music and education and other programs and ministries solely to meet the needs of those of us already in the church. If we aim solely to satisfy our own personal likes and dislikes, tastes and preferences, then as the average age of our mainline church members becomes older and older, the more we are likely to find ourselves stuck in 1955. That process, of course, becomes a vicious, self-defeating cycle.

This is not altogether, however, a generational dynamic. One encounters some amazingly traditional young adults and some incredibly open-minded, change-affirming older adults. In my first couple of years of ministry at East Liberty I called on a member who was then into her early nineties. (She is still living and going strong at one hundred and five!) As I was leaving her apartment she said, "I wonder if you would be interested in a book that was one of my husband's favorites, a book that makes me think of you." The book she handed me was *Self-Renewal* by John Gardner, published back in 1963. I devoured it! If that book had been required reading in our seminaries and business schools when it first came out, our churches and business organizations might not have been in the predicaments that many have experienced over the intervening years. Here, for example, is what Gardner had to say in 1963 about the use of our resources, financial and otherwise:

> A mature society must make a particular effort to reward its innovators, because its very maturity discourages innovation. . . . It is not so much a question of possessions as of the attitude one takes toward them. If affluent individuals (societies) commit themselves unreservedly to the conservation of their resources, affluence can be a deadening force. But if they regard their resources as providing a wide margin within which they can enjoy the luxury of creative experimentation with their environment, affluence can be a blessing. . . . Few understand how essential . . . flexibility is for continuous renewal. Assets committed to the goal of continuous renewal will never be a burden.[1]

Flexibility, creative experimentation, innovation, risk taking, continuous renewal—sounds sort of entrepreneurial, doesn't it? Like the parable of the talents, with the same promise and the same warning.

4

Signs of Pentecost

Visions of an Inclusive,
Spirit-filled Church

The minute I stepped into the pulpit of East Liberty that first Sunday, it felt like home. I had a deep sense of conviction that I was right where God meant me to be, and on the very day that God meant me to be there. It seemed providential that this "candidating" sermon, the sermon after which the congregation would vote yes or no on my call to serve as their senior pastor, was on Pentecost Sunday.

The first Pentecost, of course, was that Jewish festival day, fifty days after the resurrection of Christ, when the Holy Spirit was poured out upon the waiting disciples of Christ. Moved by the Spirit to proclaim the gospel of Christ to the multitude of Jews gathered in Jerusalem from many nations, the disciples were amazed to discover that God had gifted them with the ability to speak in a universal language. Foreigners of various nations and diverse tongues—all could hear and understand the Gospel as if it were being proclaimed in their native language. In explaining this event to the assembled crowd, the apostle Peter drew upon these verses from the prophet Joel and proclaimed that Joel's prophecy was now being fulfilled:

> In the last days it will be, God declares,
> that I will pour out my Spirit upon all flesh,
>   and your sons and your daughters shall prophesy,
> and your young men shall see visions,
>   and your old men shall dream dreams.
> Even upon my slaves, both men and women,
>   in those days I will pour out my Spirit;
>   and they shall prophesy.

(Acts 2:17–18)

That was a powerful biblical vision of a diverse and inclusive faith community—men and women, young and old, slaves and those who had slaves—all being granted equal access to the visions and dreams inspired by the Spirit of God. As much as any other single factor, it was the diversity and inclusivity of East Liberty Presbyterian Church that had attracted me to this unique congregation. I knew of no other Presbyterian congregation anywhere that included such a rich mixture of black and white, rich and poor, urbanites and suburbanites, people from all walks of life. Here was a church that was already well along the way toward living out the Pentecostal vision.

So, drawing on the account of Pentecost in chapter 2 of Acts, I said to the congregation: Here are three outstanding characteristics of the Christian church we see the Holy Spirit forming in the very beginning. First of all, as we have emphasized, it was a diverse and inclusive community of faith. Second, the early church depicted in Acts was a caring, loving, sharing community. Its members took care of one another, shared their possessions with one another, shared common meals, worshiped and prayed and studied the faith together, grew together in their common faith and love. Third, the church that was filled with God's Spirit at Pentecost was a mission church. It did not hoard the good gifts of God. It did not just care for its own. It was an outreaching, serving, giving, growing, expanding church. Like Jesus, its members reached out to heal the sick and feed the hungry. By word and deed these early Christians spread the good news of God's love in Christ. Gladly and graciously they opened their arms to newcomers in the faith. They welcomed new members, baptized them and nurtured them as disciples of Christ in the way of Christ.

Inclusive, caring, committed to mission and service, growing in numbers and in spirit—that's the vision proclaimed and affirmed in my candidating sermon on that Pentecost Sunday in 1988. This is also, I said to the congregation, the kind of church that I see you being and becoming. If you see what I see, then let's pray for that same Spirit to fill us and work in us. Let's join hands and hearts and build this Pentecostal church together. That was the vision, that was the call that I prayed the congregation was endorsing when, at the congregational meeting that followed the service, they voted to call me as their new senior pastor.

Developing a Strategy
to Build an Inclusive Church

How was it going to work? How would it be possible to continue building on the congregation's present diversity without the church eventually becoming either/or rather than both/and, to continue becoming *both* black *and* white, *both* inner city *and* metropolitan?

First of all, it seemed necessary in the beginning to keep on affirming and communicating again and again a positive self-image of the congregation. Decades of membership decline together with numerous disputes in the church had produced considerable demoralization. Some members and leaders could only remember the glory days long gone and bemoan their passing. Many seemed unable to appreciate the church's present strengths and its future potential. Others were in denial about the seriousness of its present condition.

I soon learned that there were those members, including some in leadership positions, who saw as liabilities those very aspects of the congregation's present life and ministry that I saw as assets and opportunities: the church's location in a predominantly black, inner-city neighborhood; the increasing numbers of neighborhood people coming into the congregation; the presence of a homeless men's shelter in the church; the presence of all kinds of people in the worshiping congregation.

My approach was to make clear from the very start a commitment to the neighborhood and to the African American presence in the community and in the church. The preacher for my installation service was a longtime friend from the Chicago area, an African American clergywoman. With both the senior pastor search committee and the associate pastors search committee that was organized in the fall of 1988, I shared my strong view that aiming for racial and gender inclusivity on the professional church staff needed to be a high priority. Not everyone was convinced.

A two-pronged strategy made good sense to me. First, we should continue to utilize the church's many community outreach programs as primary vehicles for drawing new people from the neighborhood into the church. Many congregations in urban situations such as East Liberty keep their community outreach programs and the participants in those programs at arm's length. They extend no clear welcome to those who have no other church home to join in the whole life of the congregation. East Liberty, with its annual community dinners and other signs of welcome to neighborhood people, was already moving in the right direction. A few men from the homeless shelter had joined the church. Daughters of Zipporah, a church-sponsored support group for single mothers on welfare, was beginning to bring a few of its members into the wider life of the congregation. We only needed to make our efforts more intentional: gathering mailing lists from the many community groups meeting in our church to send their members invitations to participate in churchwide activities and programs, and sending church staff members to their meetings to extend similar messages of welcome.

The second prong of our strategy could be realized through advertising campaigns that would reach out to the whole metropolitan area. We could begin to project new images of the church—different from the old, outdated "Mellon Church" image that still lingered in many Pittsburgh minds—images that would attract new people with fresh ideas from all over the region.

Through a local Pittsburgh ad agency, our membership committee began to develop a series of print media image ads that would appeal to those we identified as our natural target market. Target markets is more accurate. As a diverse, inclusive congregation, we wanted our advertising to be directed at several different populations simultaneously. Generally speaking, we believed that we could draw new people who would be attracted to:

a mixed-race and socially diverse congregation that offered a warm welcome to all;

a congregation that combined mission outreach in its urban neighborhood with an active concern for peace and justice worldwide;

a congregation that nurtured thinking as well as feeling approaches to faith;

a congregation sensitive to young adults and their concerns;

a congregation ready and willing to tackle the tough issues of the day.

Providentially, a young man in his mid-thirties on the staff of that ad agency was immediately drawn to our congregation. He entered fully into our congregational life and then, combining his sense of who we were with what he thought would appeal to the sorts of people who would be attracted to our kind of church, he helped us develop four very different, very effective ads. Our ads (see Appendix) appeared not in the religion sections but in the weekend entertainment sections of Pittsburgh's two daily papers, in a weekly free entertainment paper directed to young adults, and in university campus papers.

Our advertising strategy was to combine image ads with the promotion of special events, so each of our image ads also carried a few tag lines at the bottom promoting an upcoming special event in the life of the church. This allowed us to gauge the impact of our advertising by comparing, for example, the number of those attending an advertised Christmas service with the average attendance at similar unadvertised events in recent years.

Truth in Advertising

Over time, advertising continues to be effective only so long as the product actually delivers. Word of mouth is also a powerful advertising medium. If a church that claims to welcome and understand young adults doesn't actually follow through when young adults turn up, then they and others with whom they share their experiences won't continue to show up. If a church that claims to be warm and friendly actually turns a cold shoulder to newcomers, leaving them standing alone and uncomfortable at after-service coffee hours, advertising dollars are soon a waste of money. If we claimed to be a church that welcomed both blacks and whites, but the cultural preferences of whites clearly prevailed, then we had misrepresented ourselves.

Some of our people worried about such matters when we first started our advertising efforts. Did we really have the goods? Would newcomers show up only to find a depressed and dying church? My job was to keep affirming that we already had a lot going for us. We had a unique organization of volunteers called the Care Bearers. This dedicated group reached out by phone calls and personal notes to let absentee members know they were missed. Care Bearers also kept on the alert at worship services to identify and welcome newcomers. In addition, we had interim staff and, eventually, permanent professional staff members assigned to write and phone visitors, to get acquainted with them and their interests, to inform them of opportunities for involvement and invite their participation. From the start, all of us involved in membership growth efforts shared the view that we should aim to be friendly and welcoming to newcomers without overdoing it. A spirit of genuine hospitality was to prevail. As one newcomer who became a member put it, "You're friendly, but not *too* friendly."

In the area of mission outreach, we clearly had plenty of opportunities for volunteer service right in our own building to offer mission-minded newcomers to the church: working with the homeless shelter, the soup kitchen, the tutoring programs. We also had a justice and global concerns committee offering frequent classes and workshops on international peace and justice issues.

The two new associate pastors who joined our staff in early 1990 promised to bring new strengths to our efforts to live up to our advertising claims. One was a black South African with a Ph.D. from a prestigious American seminary and four years of experience in an inner-city pastorate. He was to be our associate for community mission, justice and global concerns. The other associate, a white female with ten years' experience in urban churches, quickly proved quite effective in reaching out and relating to young adults. She would serve as associate for membership growth and care. We were off and running, it seemed, with what some of us were calling our "dream team for the '90s."

One area that was an early and growing concern for me, however, was our failure to be truly multicultural in our worship and music. True, we did offer two alternatives to our traditional 11:00 A.M. worship service. The 8:00 A.M. Sunday service featured stirring, old-time gospel hymns and songs combined with opportunities for personal testimony and shared prayer concerns. That service, however, was designed principally for men in the homeless shelter. A dedicated handful of members who were committed to the shelter ministry also attended the service, but the hour was too early and the service's location in the shelter area of the building was too remote to be effective in attracting new visitors to the church. In addition, at 9:00 A.M. on Sunday there was a half-hour service of Holy Communion. While it was small and informal, the liturgy and music at this service was still largely traditional. The two dozen or so folk who regularly attended were mostly elderly.

Sanctuary worship at 11:00 A.M. was quite formal and even a bit high-church for Presbyterians. The music was consistently drawn from the classical Eurocentric sacred music tradition, much of it from the Anglican cathedral sources. It was beautiful music and consistently well performed, but I was increasingly doubtful that the overall repertoire was right for who we were and where we were as a congregation—right, perhaps, for this church and this community in the '50s, but not in the '90s.

When I reported to the church's longtime organist and music director that I had heard some complaints that too many of his choral selections were in Latin, he came back to me a bit later to report that during the previous year only 14 percent of his selections were in Latin. When I advanced the ideal of becoming more multicultural in our musical selections, he replied that our music was already multicultural since it included composers from England, France, Germany, Austria, Italy, and so on. When, at one of our staff meetings, he expressed his longing for the good old days when our ushers wore morning coats with long tails and striped pants, I protested, "But that's a class statement." To which he replied with an absolutely straight face, "You're darn tooting it is!"

I knew when I began my ministry at East Liberty that this particular staff member had been there already sixteen years before me. I was also told that he and "his" choir were major influences in the departure of my predecessor after just four years. (Some years later, one of the younger choir members told me that on the day of my installation service, one of the longtime choir members leaned over to him and said, "Well, here we go again, another senior pastor for us to break in.") Aware that the music director had five years to go until he was sixty-five and that he had given indications of planning to retire then, I made a political decision to bite that particular bullet and wait it out for five years. I also continued to worry a great deal about what on earth we might be able to do in the meantime about our worship and music life—about this very central and very visible inconsistency between, on the one hand, our present practice, and on the other hand, our vision of becoming a truly multicultural congregation.

5

Drinking from Strange Wells

Enculturating the Gospel

I was having second thoughts about this particular piece of junk mail, so I had to retrieve it from the wastebasket. God can speak to us in many different ways, sometimes even through junk mail. Maybe this one was a message I needed to heed. It came from a congregation in Phoenix called the Community Church of Joy, and it announced their Academy of Church Growth, to be held the week after Easter of 1991.

It was the fact that their featured musical artist for this event was Debby Boone that had initially prompted me to toss the piece in the trash. But another little voice said to me, "Hold on a minute! Are you being closed-minded here? Are you letting yourself be controlled by the same sort of rigid stereotyping and cultural snobbery that you so often deplore in your preaching? And what about the fact that the Community Church of Joy is apparently a successfully innovative and rapidly growing mainline congregation affiliated with the largest Lutheran denomination in the United States? Maybe you could learn something from them." So I sent in my registration and flew to Phoenix.

On the face of it the Community of Joy and East Liberty Presbyterian Church could not have been more dissimilar. The former was located in the white suburbs of a rapidly growing, sun-belt metropolitan area. Their membership was virtually all-white, middle-class, younger families. Their theology tended toward evangelical conservatism. What on earth could they teach an inner-city, racially mixed, older congregation in a declining, rust-belt city with a commitment to being multicultural and a tradition of being theologically moderate to liberal? What could we learn from them? A good deal, as it turned out.

"Enculturating the Gospel" was one of the big lessons that the Joy Academy of Church Growth had to teach. Ever since my divinity school days, when I headed a storefront mission on the back side of Beacon Hill in Boston, I had been committed to enculturating the gospel—offering the good news to the people we're trying to reach in terms and forms that relate to their situation, that speak to them in their language and their cultural style, addressing their existential questions. As the Joy Academy pointed out, however, while we learned long ago the importance of enculturating the gospel in overseas missionary work, we have often failed to practice it at home. We have museum churches offering an antique culture that seems either humorously quaint or weird and off-putting to the unchurched who have not grown up with it, often even to our own young adults who *have* grown up with it. We continue singing hymns, for example, with dated language that most people haven't heard spoken in their lifetime, conveying messages that often seem badly out of touch even to the average churchgoer.

Another point that became much clearer to me after three days at the Joy Academy was that theological conservatism does not necessarily lead to a practical conservatism, nor theological liberalism to a practical liberalism. Here were theological conservatives ready and willing to experiment, to innovate, to depart from traditional language and traditional worship forms in order to reach out with the gospel to those who would otherwise be turned off and turned away by those traditions. There was no hard sell evangelism here, no off-putting talk of "saving the lost" or "winning souls for Christ," no altar calls or testimonies. Conservatives, it seems, tend to be more rigid about scriptural interpretation and doctrine, more open about worship and music styles, while the reverse is true of liberals. Would that we could begin to learn a bit from one another.

At the Joy Academy bookstore I picked up a copy of a book that I would certainly have ignored previously, a book by the pastor of a Foursquare Gospel Church in Seattle. *The Baby Boomerang: Catching the Baby Boomers as They Come Back to Church,* by Doug Murren, was another eye-opener.[1] Now I could see why churches like his were growing while churches like mine were dying. Here was a man truly open to contemporary secular culture and its trends—a man ready and willing, on the one hand, to speak to that culture in its own terms in order to reach people yearning for faith and spiritual healing, and on the other hand, to challenge secular culture and his own faith tradition where they needed challenging. And all the time I had been thinking that his kind of faith was supposed to be closed-minded and rigid while my kind of faith was supposed to be open-minded and flexible!

I had to admit to myself that, by comparison, many of the moderate to liberal Christians I knew were exceedingly set in their ways—about, for example, forms of worship and classical sacred music traditions—ready and willing to go down with a sinking ship so long as there was no abandonment or compromise of their very class-determined musical preferences. And a sinking ship it might well be, since, as I learned at the Joy Academy, classical music represents no more than 4 percent of recorded music sales in the United States today.

I also came away from the Joy Academy and the reading of Doug Murren's book with a much clearer realization that being truly multicultural has to do with more than affirming and embracing race and class and ethnic differences.

It also has to do with affirming and embracing generational differences. If it is true that musical tastes and preference are today one of the prime indicators of cultural differences, then it is necessary to understand that between a white, middle-class twenty-year-old and a white, middle-class fifty-year-old there may be wide cultural gaps just as relevant to our church life as are the cultural differences between races, social classes, and ethnic groups. And if this is so, then it is also apparent that we mainline Protestants have been as indifferent to enculturating the gospel for our own children and grandchildren as we have for any other cultural group.

Practical Guidance

Relevant, practical lessons garnered from the Joy Academy about the kind of worship that is designed to reach an unchurched, younger generation included these ten points:

1. Recognize that worship is first base, your prime-time recruitment opportunity. This is where you are going to reach most newcomers and prospective new members.
2. Plan worship with the people you are trying to reach uppermost in your heart and mind. Consider what kind of language, music, participation will speak to them, will make them feel comfortable and at home.
3. Remember that many unchurched people have had no formal religious training or experience. They probably don't know what a "Gloria Patri" or "narthex" or "undercroft" is, may not even know the words to the Lord's Prayer. Take nothing for granted. Make your service user-friendly for the unchurched.
4. Avoid being a "museum church" with a "period-piece culture." Remember that classical music and liturgical worship are off-putting to many younger adults.
5. Don't make a big deal of your denominational identity. People are not looking for this today and many find it a big turnoff.
6. Preach what is practical and relevant to everyday life. Deal with concerns of work, marriage and family life, friendship, sex, depression, aging, and so on. Offer people encouragement and hope.
7. Remember that young adults who don't attend church say that they stay away because they find it boring, dull, slow-paced, and irrelevant.
8. Don't try to blend or alternate contemporary and traditional worship at one and the same service. Nobody will be happy. Keep your traditional service, but offer a new, contemporary alternative service. [Later we will have reason to qualify this point.]

9. Modify your traditional, liturgical service to:
   a. Pick up the pace, cut out the dead spots.
   b. Begin the service with an uplift—a stirring introit or joyful hymn.
   c. Make the service a celebration.
   d. Assure that greeters and ushers are well-trained.
   e. Have musicians up-front and well-amplified.
   f. Offer some moments of informality and humor.
   g. Explain your terminology.
10. Remember that a warm and loving, open and welcoming environment is absolutely essential.

I was impressed with the Rev. Walt Kallestad, senior pastor of the Community Church of Joy, a man at once humble and visionary. Toward the end of the conference, Kallestad referred to the need we sometimes have on our spiritual journey to "drink from strange wells." That spoke to me. It had been something of a stretch for me to attend the Joy Academy of Church Growth. It had, indeed, been like drinking from a strange well. Yet I was leaving with the good feeling that I had been both challenged and refreshed. I wasn't going back to Pittsburgh ready to recommend that we invite Debby Boone to East Liberty as a guest musician, but I was going home with plenty to ponder about possible future directions for our worship and music life. In entrepreneurial terms, I had learned a great deal from the "competition."

Pulling an End Run

Given the stance of our longtime music director, of most of our choir members, and of our worship and music committee on which the music director and a number of his choir members sat, I knew it was going to be virtually impossible to encourage a truly open exploration of these learnings as I returned home. I did, nevertheless, make presentations both to the worship and music committee and to the session about the lessons of my Joy Academy experience. There were some positive, even enthusiastic responses, but it still seemed politically counterproductive to press any sort of all-out, frontal assault for an 11:00 A.M. service change.

Still, there were constructive steps that could be taken. Some, in fact, we were already taking. We were already trying to practice most of the nonmusical points included in the ten-point outline above. In addition, our membership and growth committee was undertaking certain musical initiatives that our worship and music committee could not or would not. Because the membership and growth committee had special funds for special events to draw new people and increase our membership, we had already begun to use some of these funds to bring in outside groups to offer music in the sanctuary for fifteen to twenty minutes prior to the beginning of the 11:00 A.M. service. Without seeking an opinion from the director of music, on Martin Luther King Jr. Sunday we hosted the Sounds of Heritage, a fine Pittsburgh African American musical group dedicated to preserving and promoting the tradition of Negro spirituals. Observing February as Black History Month, we featured Umoja, an African drum and dance group from the University of Pittsburgh. We also hosted in this pre-service slot a touring band of homeless men from Harlem. It would have been awkward for anyone to complain openly about our hosting these black organizations in a congregation that was now welcoming an increasing number of black members. There was, of course, some grumbling behind the scenes.

Being realistic, we knew that the most feasible and appropriate new direction in worship and music for us appeared to be in initiating new developments outside our traditional worship service. Our worship and music traditionalists didn't seem much to care about what went on outside of Sunday at 11:00 A.M. An evening hour, however, seemed out of the question on account of the security concerns that prevent many people, especially new people, from venturing into our inner-city area after dark. But what about our Sunday morning schedule? What if we combined our 8:00 A.M. Good Samaritan Homeless Shelter service and our traditional 8:45 A.M. service of Holy Communion into one informal service that featured gospel music? So we tried putting these two together in one early service held outdoors in our church courtyard in the summer of 1991. We called it the Service of Joy.

Sadly, there were too many obstacles to overcome and this venture proved short-lived. The hour was too early to attract many newcomers, especially the young. The older, traditional members who attended the previous 8:45 A.M. Communion service did not take to the informality or the gospel music of the new service. Those responsible for planning the former Good Samaritan worship felt that the homeless men and their needs were being downplayed in the new service, that the men couldn't be themselves as freely in this new mix of people as they had been in their own worship. So after a period of evaluation, the joint service was dropped and the Good Samaritan service returned to its 8:00 A.M. time.

Having made something of a breakthrough with the other early service, however, we continued to call it the Service of Joy, and to offer a more informal, contemporary worship and music style. We moved that service to an 8:45 A.M. time slot. While we did lose some of the older people who had previously preferred that service, the changes in music and style resulted in doubling the average attendance.

At the same time, in a move intended to be reassuring to traditionalists, to make the best use of the strengths of our music director and choir, and to promote church growth, our membership and growth committee proposed making funds available for members of the Pittsburgh Symphony Orchestra to accompany our choir and organ in presenting Christmas portions of Handel's *Messiah* during our 11:00 A.M. service on the Sunday before Christmas in 1991. That service was well publicized and attendance was by far the largest of any East

Liberty service in many, many years—878. It also demonstrated that all was not lost concerning the drawing power of classical sacred music.

What would turn out to be the most successful worship and music innovation of my first decade at ELPC was still, however, yet to be initiated. As 1991 came to a close, the next step was still only a dream born in the minds of two people during a pilgrimage to France that previous summer.

6

A Pilgrimage of Trust

Taizé—Another Strange Well

The brothers of the ecumenical monastic community located in the tiny French village of Taizé periodically "take their show on the road" to other lands. They call it a "pilgrimage of trust." Each international Taizé prayer meeting is just that, both for the brothers who sponsor these massive assemblies and for those who attend—mostly young adults by the thousands, sometimes tens of thousands, even hundreds of thousands. By U.S. standards, planning and organization for these events seem minimal, even haphazard. Housing for pilgrims is provided in the homes of church members in host cities. Meal arrangements are rather ad hoc. Sometimes additional meeting space and housing are needed at the last minute because thousands more have come than were expected. Yet, somehow, the pilgrimage of trust always works.

The whole history of the Taizé community has been a pilgrimage of trust. Begun toward the end of World War II by Roger Schutz of the Swiss Reformed Church, the church of John Calvin, this was the first (and is still the only) monastic community ever founded by a member of the Reformed faith. Brother Roger's vision was to form a community for both Protestant and Catholic brothers as a witness to Christian unity, a living parable of ecumenical community. And that it has become. It is today the world's only ecumenical monastic order, officially recognized by the Vatican, with a Protestant founder and prior. Brother Roger and his first small band of brothers initially envisioned a quiet, meditative life in the peaceful countryside of Burgundy. But God seemed to have other plans. As the brothers composed their own unique prayer chants, simple yet haunting prayer songs sung three times daily, a steadily increasing stream of young adults from near and far began arriving in Taizé. Here were unexpected, uninvited pilgrims, seeking to share these beautifully peaceful and spiritually calming prayer songs with the brothers. The tide of visitors swelled to thousands weekly, especially during holiday breaks and in the summer. The brothers were hard-pressed to provide food and lodging. But somehow barracks were erected, tents were provided, kitchens were enlarged, and the chapel was expanded. Gone was the quiet and meditative solitude the brothers had envisioned for themselves, yet they willingly accepted this new worldwide ministry to spiritually hungry, young adult seekers whom God had brought to their doorstep. The brothers' pilgrimage of trust had taken a new, unexpected direction.

I had heard of Taizé in the early 1960s while a student at Harvard Divinity School. I read the writings of some of the brothers who were Bible scholars and theologians, aware that they were making significant contributions to exciting new breakthroughs in Protestant-Catholic relations. In the mid-1980s I was captivated by the Taizé music that our youth music director began introducing to our congregation in Evanston. Later, after we had been in Pittsburgh a couple of years, my wife and I heard enthusiastic reports from a member of our former congregation who had spent a week in Taizé during the spring of 1990. Feeling drawn to experience Taizé for ourselves, Jan and I began to make plans for a two-week trip to France in July of 1991.

In the Dark

Just a few weeks before we were to depart for France, our East Liberty faith journey was jolted by a sudden, frightening turn. Within the space of just a few days, several women in the congregation, individually and independently of one another, came forward with accounts of their having been the target of unwelcome sexual advances from our new male associate pastor. He had been with us just fifteen months at that point. When confronted, he responded with total denial and counteraccusations of wrongdoing against his accusers. He even raged openly about the matter with highly inappropriate remarks in a sermon he preached the next Sunday. It was clear that he was ready and willing to do battle, dividing the congregation into warring camps.

Following guidelines on the proper handling of reports of sexual misconduct that had been adopted by our Presbyterian General Assembly just a few weeks previously, I had initially made a painful but prompt decision to report the first accusations to officials of the Presbytery of Pittsburgh. (Clergy misconduct in the Presbyterian system is the responsibility of the presbytery rather than of the local church session.) Alarmed by the accused associate's inflammatory sermon, and following the advice of presbytery officials, the East Liberty session quickly voted to place him on an indefinite administrative leave—with full pay. The presbytery would now appoint an investigative committee to determine if charges should be brought. If so, presbytery would then conduct an ecclesiastical trial.

In the meantime, we were strongly counseled by presbytery officials, as well as by our congregation's legal advisers, to say as little as possible to anyone about what was transpiring. The congregation, in effect, was to be left in the dark for an undetermined period of time. And all of this was coming just a few months after our session had decided to embark on a major fund-raising effort in the fall of 1991. We would be seeking a major boost in giving through three-year pledges from our members in support of an effort we had tagged—quite presciently, in retrospect—as "Our Courageous Commitment Campaign."

I was devastated, anxious, and demoralized. What did the future hold for those women of our congregation who had felt morally obligated to come forward with their difficult accounts of a minister's alleged offenses? For our associate? For his wife and their three school-age children? What would this mean for our congregation, especially for race relations, for our ability to continue building a multiracial congregation? Where on earth was the hand of God in any of this? Things had been developing so well according to plan and with so much promise for East Liberty. All our efforts and accomplishments could be demolished, all our hopes and dreams brought to nothing by this tragic and potentially destructive turn of events.

Immediately Jan and I faced a difficult decision about our trip to France. Was it foolish, considering what was happening and all that might happen in our absence, to continue with our travel plans? Friends and advisers encouraged us to go. Matters were now in the hands of presbytery. Little or nothing could be accomplished by abandoning our plans and staying home. The time away, the distance might be just what we needed at this point. That advice seemed sound, so we decided to go ahead on what was turning out to be truly a pilgrimage of trust.

Light in the Darkness

It was hard for me to enjoy that first week we spent touring in central and southern France. I was still anxious and distracted, my mind back in Pittsburgh, poring over possible scenarios of disaster. The next week at Taizé, however, was, indeed, exactly what I needed. There was the beautiful, peaceful countryside. There were our plain but comfortable accommodations in a medieval cottage called "the cherry tree," about a fifteen-minute walk from Taizé down an unpaved country lane. Most important of all, there were the three daily prayer services held in the brothers' Church of Reconciliation. There I had three hours a day for a whole week to let the sung prayers of Taizé seep their healing, mesmerizing way into my heart, mind, and soul.

What is the drawing power of Taizé? Why has its simple music spread to thousands of Catholic and Protestant churches the world over? Taizé offers a spirituality and a form of worship that are hard to find elsewhere in our time. There are certainly plenty of high-energy songs of praise and joy in the Taizé collection, but many of the Taizé chants speak to the dark, downside experiences of our existence, our experiences of loss and doubt and disappointment. The services are held in semidarkness, illuminated only by candles—many candles. The simple prayer songs, sung over and over again like a mantra, are often drawn from scripture. Their messages encourage us in the dark passages of our lives to hold on in faith, to look toward the light, to trust in God whose way may presently seem obscure but whose day is surely near. Three times a day for a whole week my soul was healed as I chanted again and again and again with thousands of other pilgrims:

> Our darkness is not darkness in your sight;
> The deepest night is clear as the light.

> Wait for the Lord, whose day is near.
> Wait for the Lord, be strong, take heart.

> When the night becomes dark,
> Your love, O Lord, is a fire;
> Your love, O Lord, is a fire.
> Nothing can trouble, nothing can frighten.
> Those who seek God shall never go wanting.
> God alone fills us.[1]

Thomas Moore in his *Care of the Soul* has spoken of the soul's need for what the Taizé spiritual garden can offer—both to the individual and to the community—for those who frequent it:

> It is not a literal aberration, although it may feel that way, to suddenly find meaning and value disappear, and to be overwhelmed with the need for withdrawal and with vague emotions of hopelessness. Such feelings have a place and work a kind of magic on the soul. . . . Over time something essential emerges . . . the gold in the sludge. We may find it exhausting trying to keep life bright and warm at all costs. We may even be more overcome then by the increased melancholy. Some Renaissance gardens had a bower dedicated to Saturn—a dark, shaded, remote place where a person could retire and enter the persona of depression without fear of being disturbed. . . . Because depression is one of the faces of the soul, acknowledging it and bringing it into our relationships fosters intimacy. If we deny or cover up anything that is at home in the soul, then we cannot be fully present to others. Hiding the dark places results in a loss of soul; speaking for them and from them offers a way toward genuine community and intimacy.[2]

Some older readers might wonder how such an emphasis on difficulty, darkness, and doubt could possibly appeal to young adults. Musically, of course, there is the sometimes almost demonic darkness of Generation X's "gothic rock." A moment's further reflection, moreover, will remind us that youth suicide rates in the Western world have never been so high as in recent decades. Growing up in a world of planetary destruction, increasing and deadly disparities between the world's rich and poor, materialism and consumerism run amuck in the Western world, our cultures plagued with violence, deadly drugs, and sometimes deadly sex, is it any wonder our youth too need a spiritual context for grief and lament?

Taizé meets another spiritual need that is often neglected by the traditional worship of our mainline churches, the need to seek, to experience, to express a personal, I-Thou relationship with the living God. Many of the Taizé prayer songs are in the first person singular, contrary to what has so often been drilled into us in the Presbyterian and Reformed tradition, that our corporate worship should always be in the first person plural rather than the first person singular. In prayer and in song we must declare that "we" praise "our" God and confess "our" sins, no "I" or "my" anything. Taizé, however, has us singing and praying the words spoken to Jesus by the thief on an adjacent cross, "Jesus, remember me when you come into your kingdom." And:

> My soul is at rest in God alone;
> My salvation comes from God.
> The Lord is my rock and my salvation.
> Whom shall I fear, whom shall I fear?

My tradition often seems afraid to affirm the nearness of God. Our worship must consistently emphasize the transcendence of God. Reformed and Presbyterian Christianity has been and typically remains suspicious of personal religious experiences and expressions as dangerously sentimental and self-centered. Thus we are frequently reminded that when Jesus taught us how to pray, he taught us to pray "*our* Father." True enough. But how about that other all-time favorite—the Twenty-third Psalm? "The LORD is *my* shepherd. *I* shall not want. . . . he leads *me* beside still waters; he restores *my* soul." Get it?

We mainline spiritual leaders had better get it before it's too late. I firmly believe that, as much as any other single factor, this one accounts for our decline and for the rapid growth of Pentecostal expressions of Christianity that offer opportunities for personal encounter with a living Spirit who works personal healing and transformation in individual lives. We need to get beyond either/or thinking on this subject. It's both/and that we're dealing with here. We need worship that celebrates both God's transcendence and God's intimate presence with us.

Jan and I were also blessed at Taizé to meet and talk several times with one of the good brothers—a gentle, empathetic good listener to whom we could pour out some of our present trials and troubles. When he heard that we were from Pittsburgh, he told us that a couple of the brothers would probably be visiting Pittsburgh in the fall to help spread the word and prepare the way for a pilgrimage of trust in Dayton, Ohio, the following spring. We were delighted and promptly offered the East Liberty Church as a gathering place if they wished to hold a Taizé prayer service in Pittsburgh to help promote the Dayton gathering.

Our Taizé pilgrimage had restored and renewed our faith. And it would sustain us through the difficult months ahead. As the summer passed and we moved on into fall, the presbytery investigation into charges against our associate pastor also wore on with no end in sight. In fact, through the summer and into the fall, more persons had come forward with additional charges against him. Once again, my spirits began to sag.

Once again, Taizé lifted us up. Brothers were indeed coming to Pittsburgh. They wanted to use our church for a gathering in October. With wonderful support from the musicians of St. Paul's monastery in Pittsburgh, a marvelous Taizé evening service was held at East Liberty Church with five hundred worshipers in attendance, Protestants and Catholics together from all over the region. In addition to renewing our own spirits, that event afforded Jan and me the opportunity for which we had been yearning to share our Taizé experience with interested members of our congregation. That service also gave us the spiritual sustenance we were going to need for our continuing pilgrimage of faith through the next four difficult months to come.

Finally, I need to underline one of the most important personal spiritual lessons that I have learned anew from the spirituality of Taizé. I am a dreamer and a planner, very goal-oriented, focused, and intentional in my life and my work. As a teenager I recited with enthusiasm that phrase in our national Presbyterian youth organization's statement of purpose in which we committed ourselves to "discover the will of God for our lives—and do it." So when you believe with all your heart that you've discovered God's will and are trying your best to do it, it's pretty hard to handle it when your plans and projects seem derailed and defeated, your hopes and dreams shattered. This long, dark passage that began in 1991 and continued into 1992 was the most painful experience to date in my entire ministerial career of nearly thirty years.

What I learned anew from Taizé was that God's ways are not necessarily my ways, that my plans are not necessarily God's plans. Even when we're headed in the right direction, God may well have an alternative route in mind for us to get there. We have no divine guarantees that, even when we have the best of intentions, everything is going to work out as we think it should. There are bound to be unexpected and sometimes unwelcome turns on our spiritual journey. Often, of course, it is through our disappointments and difficulties that we learn the most about how we need to change and grow if we are not to wither and die. So we walk by faith, not by sight. That, after all, is precisely why the scriptures call us to live life as a pilgrimage of trust. This renewed insight would help prepare me for tougher stuff yet to come.

7

Becoming the Cathedral of Hope

Some Bad News, Some Good News

"This is either going to kill me or keep me young." That's what I said to myself and to a few confidants when I accepted the call to East Liberty Presbyterian Church. The results? It would depend on the day you asked. Compared to my previous pastorates, things here were so much more complex and unpredictable. There could be a rapid succession of wild mood swings over short periods of time. Moments of wonderful highs and great successes were coupled with times of awful lows and painful disappointments. Sometimes I would refer to us as "the Church of the Holy Roller Coaster."

In January of 1992, Pittsburgh Presbytery's investigation of misconduct charges against our associate pastor was concluded with the filing of charges in ecclesiastical court. This case was, of course, highly charged and sensitive in terms of both gender issues and race relations—even more so because it was taking place around the same time that the whole nation was following Anita Hill's sexual harassment accusations against Supreme Court nominee Clarence Thomas. Our East Liberty case was to go to trial before the presbytery's Permanent Judicial Commission. Three of the six women in our congregation who had reported his misconduct were ready and willing to testify. Of these three, two were white, one was black. The black woman was herself an ordained minister. The verdict, announced in February, was guilty as charged on all counts. The sentence was removal from the office of ordained ministry. To our chagrin, the case made the pages of the *Pittsburgh Post-Gazette.*

Although this verdict meant more pain for us all, it was also a relief to have the matter settled. Those of us who were closest to the facts of the case felt that the judgment was right and fair. Once the presbytery investigation was over, of course, we could discuss the matter within our congregation. Special meetings were scheduled to help the congregation understand and deal with what had happened. Presbytery officials came to explain the process without, of course, revealing the names of those who made the charges or in any way violating their privacy. A video on clergy sexual misconduct was viewed and discussed. After a couple of such meetings, I felt we needed more. Our session and members, however, seemed solidly of the opinion that we should now lay the matter to rest and move on.

Indeed, our ability to survive this crisis and move on was nothing short of amazing to me, all the more so because I knew that we were not altogether cohesive and content as a congregation. Beneath the surface and around the edges there were those unhappy about spending patterns and priorities, about worship and music innovations, about the overall pace and direction of change in general. I was also acutely aware that East Liberty Church had a history of harboring more than its share of troubled and troubling individuals ready and willing to seize on potential grievances and causes for complaint. However, our members and our officers—with just one glaring exception—had handled this difficult, painful episode with admirable maturity and calm.

The one exception was Judd (as we will call him), an individual who, while the investigation was still in process, took it upon himself to intervene with presbytery officials. Without any advance consultation with me or with the session, he went to presbytery offices to demand that our associate pastor be taken off his session-mandated administrative leave and returned to his duties at the church immediately. Quite properly, Judd's demand was ignored. Otherwise, our church officers and members accepted the process and the outcome with equanimity. At least openly, no suggestion of racial bias or divisiveness ever entered the discussions. It helped that there was black and white representation in the makeup both of the presbytery committee of investigation and of the Permanent Judicial Commission. Thankfully, it soon became clear that we would suffer virtually no racial fallout from this tragic episode, that our congregation's ability to continue attracting African Americans would remain unimpeded. By the end of 1991 our black membership had doubled over the previous three years and stood at 13.5 percent of the total.

Lots of Good News

We had come through this difficult period with significant accomplishments to buoy our spirits. Our Courageous Commitment Campaign had come very close to meeting its ambitious dollar goals. We had significantly increased both the number of members who pledged and the average amount pledged. In fact, we had doubled the dollar contributions of our members over the previous year! And we had taken in seventy new members in 1991, the largest number in many, many years, resulting in the first net gain of members since 1951 (when *I Love Lucy* first appeared on TV)! In addition, we had welcomed thirty new "friends of the church," an unofficial category of affiliation we have used to welcome those who are interested in participating in church life but who are, for one reason or another, not yet ready for full membership.

At the end of 1991 we celebrated a $100,000 grant from the R. K. Mellon Foundation to renovate the church's small dining room that served the homeless shelter and the soup kitchen. In the spring of 1992, we received word of yet another grant, $500,000 from the Vira I. Heinz Endowment to provide an endowment for the church's community outreach programming. We proposed to initiate a Family Resource Center to support and strengthen healthy family life in the congregation and the community. Within a year the center would be staffed by a United Methodist minister with a Ph.D. in social psychology, considerable urban ministry experience, and a strong multicultural perspective. By the end of 1993 he had Family Resource Center programs up and running with a weekly family meal program, a drop-in center for parents, and an after-school creative arts program for children and youth.

Funding the community mission position on our church staff with the Heinz Endowment grant allowed us to free up other professional staffing funds to try new things, develop new ministries. Demonstrating its willingness to experiment, our session approved a proposal to employ three new part-time professional staff members. One was a United Church of Christ minister with a master's degree from the Yale Institute of Sacred Music and the Arts. She would be responsible for trying to get a Taizé service off the ground and for developing a church and community ministry of the arts. The second part-time professional added to the church staff was my wife, Jan. She would be responsible for developing our adult education programming, for developing small groups, for ministry in the area of spiritual formation, and for staffing our justice and global concerns. Another woman in the congregation with training and experience as a social worker was employed to strengthen our outreach with older members and inactives. We called the three our interim pastoral associates.

Our new ministry ventures quickly bore fruit. Our new Taizé minister began organizing young adults and others to make the weekend pilgrimage to Dayton, Ohio, for the international Taizé assembly there in late May of 1992. She also provided Taizé music leadership for our Holy Saturday Easter Vigil in April and for our 11:00 A.M. worship service on Pentecost in early June. Before long, we were offering a weekly Taizé-style service of sung prayers in our chapel from 7:00 to 8:00 on Wednesday evenings. With less than a dozen or so present initially, the numbers would grow to around forty by the end of 1993, sometimes reaching as many as one hundred on special occasions.

With tremendous energy and enthusiasm our new Taizé minister was also rapidly building a comprehensive arts ministry within the church and community. Soon she was offering arts training and opportunities to children and youth through our new Family Resource Center, bringing Saturday ballet classes to children in cooperation with the Pittsburgh Ballet Theater School, and arranging for the Pittsburgh Symphony to perform at the church with the virtually all-black Summer Day Camp Choir of the East End Cooperative Ministries. Within less than two years, working part-time, she also had African American dance and drama groups performing and offering classes at the church. She fostered the organization of a church-based Creative Arts Group that helped with the planning and supporting of arts activities, took on a flower planting project within the community, and organized a summer community festival culminating in an outdoor community worship service on the church's front lawn. The latter would become a growing annual event with increasing community-wide participation.

Jan began to expand our adult education program with courses designed to reach out to connect the church and the community. In cooperation with our neighborhood community development corporation, East Liberty Development, Inc., we offered courses on home ownership for low- to moderate-income individuals through the Housing Recovery Program of the Urban Redevelopment Authority. Working with the Community College of Allegheny County, we also sponsored courses on community leadership, how to start a small business, and GED offerings. At the same time, the number and vitality of small groups in the church were also significantly expanded, with fifteen such groups meeting by the end of 1994.

In the area of justice and global concerns, Jan was at the forefront of our efforts to establish a sister parish relationship between East Liberty Church and a congregation in Central America. This project got off the ground in 1992 when, under the auspices of an international, ecumenical organization called Sister Parish, we were linked with a small Roman Catholic congregation in rural Guatemala. In the summer of the following year Jan and I led a group of four young adults on the first of what would become an annual ELPC delegation to visit and live with families of our sister parish in the village of San Francisco, Guatemala.

Favorable publicity was boosting our morale and spreading the word about our congregation. In 1991 the urban entertainment weekly *In Pittsburgh* sent a writer to cover a Muslim-Christian dialogue we sponsored. Later that year, in their annual "Best of Pittsburgh" issue the publication awarded us distinction as "Pittsburgh's Most Open-Minded Church." In 1992 another *In Pittsburgh* writer, a "church critic" who visited various church services in the city and then reviewed them either in the paper or over the airwaves on Pittsburgh's FM classical music station, gave us a rave review. "So," he concluded, "this grand church, true as ever to God's Word, is reaching out to involve people in the arts, in multiple styles of worship, in tutoring programs, in family counseling, in care for the young and old, in community action, in global concern for peace and justice. Here people join hands with all the tribes of God's children. . . . I believe this Cathedral of Hope is unique, a diamond which can be the benchmark for all once-fading inner-city churches to follow when God inspires them to a renaissance."

Thinking outside the Box,
Coloring outside the Lines

"Do you promise to serve the people with energy, intelligence, imagination, and love?" This is my favorite of all the ordination vows to which Presbyterian ministers, elders, and deacons are asked to assent. It is also the way I would characterize the two-year period from the spring of 1992 to the spring of 1994 at East Liberty Church, a time of exciting innovation, creative experimentation, and stimulating vitality. It was during this period that we began, with greater and greater frequency, to call ourselves the Cathedral of Hope, placing less emphasis on denominational identity and more emphasis on what we were offering to the community at large. In early 1992 we initiated a rather bold strategic planning process that was completed by mid-1994. Also during this time, we were offering an increasing variety in worship and music, including the first of several annual appearances of the African Children's Choir that filled our sanctuary with largely African American visitors at our 11:00 A.M. worship. There were 754 present at the first one in 1992, then 1,262 in 1993, and 1,220 in 1994!

The results were showing in membership growth figures. In 1993 we received 103 new members and friends, 39 of whom were under thirty-five years of age and 38 of whom were between thirty-six and fifty. They came from 21 different zip codes. Twenty-seven were either in graduate school or held graduate degrees. An additional 26 had some college or a college degree. About one-third were African American. By the end of 1993 our membership had become nearly 19 percent African American. The growth pattern was similar in 1994: 98 new members and friends from 24 zip codes and 5 foreign countries.

In so many ways, the growing sense of excitement and vitality in the church during this period must be attributed to the willingness of staff and lay leaders alike to think outside the box, to color outside the lines. Nancy Ammerman has observed in her landmark study of congregations in changing communities, *Congregation and Community*, that those congregations she studied that were able to adapt to change and to thrive in new circumstances were those blessed with strong pastors who could envision and lead the way to new possibilities. But just as essential, she notes, are "responsive, imaginative, and energetic lay persons willing to participate in the necessary processes of change and to alter a rewarding [i.e., for them] pattern of involvements for something they hope will be better."[1]

Our leadership's willingness to move beyond denominational boundaries was one example of adaptation and change that our leaders were willing to make in this period. We now had two ministers from other denominations on our staff. For other professional staff positions we had co-opted able lay leaders from within the congregation. We were also moving beyond the confines of denominational tradition by offering music and worship styles not customarily identified as Presbyterian. The Taizé service featured chanting, long periods of silences, icons, and lots of candles. The Service of Joy welcomed visiting choirs and soloists from black Baptist churches, jazz bands, and monthly circle dancing as part of worship. We added billboards to our advertising mix, with billboards for our Service of Joy that proclaimed, "The Joint Is Jumpin'!"

We were resisting the easy path of identifying one demographically homogenous target market for our church by intentionally reaching out to diverse populations. Unlike many mainline churches, we saw no reason that our multiple worship services needed to be identical to one another in style and content. Quite the contrary, we felt called to offer worship experiences to meet as wide a range of needs and tastes as we possibly could.

Other more or less risky developments in this period included our session's vote to cosponsor an ecumenical fellowship group for gays and lesbians initiated by a neighboring United Methodist Church. An adult series was offered on "Understanding Sexual Orientation" and a support group was organized around the same concern. In 1991 I preached a sermon series on sexual morality in which I took a positive approach to committed same-sex relationships. In 1993 I offered a series entitled "Timely Talks on Ten Tough Topics." The topics included such issues as sexual morality, abortion, euthanasia, gender equality, and inclusive language.

By and large the congregation was supportive of preaching that not infrequently touched on controversial subjects. From time to time, my sermons challenged U.S. foreign policy in Central America, the Gulf War, and economic and racial inequalities in the United States. Together with the Thomas Merton Center of Pittsburgh, our justice and global concerns committee cosponsored a poetry reading by Ernesto Cardenal, minister of culture in the Sandinista government of Nicaragua. I did once during this period get a literal red flag. Coming home one day in 1990, I found that some secret admirer had left a gift at our front door—a big, resplendently red Soviet flag, emblazoned with gold hammer and sickle!

The kind of new people we were attracting were, for the most part, curious and open-minded, stimulated by an environment where controversial topics were not off-limits, where traditional beliefs and practices could be questioned, where risk taking was expected. One of the most significant and consequential steps that we took in reaching out to such people came in October of 1993. It was an invitation extended by our membership and growth committee to controversial Roman Catholic theologian Matthew Fox to lecture, lead a Saturday workshop, and preach at our 11:00 A.M. service on Reformation Sunday.

PART II

Building and Battling

Then the Lord answered me and said:
Write the vision;
   make it plain on tablets,
   so that a runner may read it.

                      —Habakkuk 2:2

And each of the builders had his sword strapped at
his side while he built.

                      —Nehemiah 4:18

8

Reaching a Generation of Seekers

Welcoming Spiritually Homeless Strangers

"Show hospitality toward strangers," enjoins the letter to the Hebrews, "for by doing that some have entertained angels without knowing it" (Heb.13:2). Jesus himself said, "I was a stranger and you welcomed me" (Matt. 25:35). Jesus, in fact, never ceases challenging us to take risks in reaching out to share God's love. "I was hungry and you fed me," he said, "homeless and you took me in." For risk-taking mainline churches that are ready and willing to reach out and connect with strangers who are spiritually hungry and spiritually homeless there is a mission field that, again in the words of Jesus, is "white unto harvest." For several years the signs have been all around us, plain as can be out there in our supposedly secular culture. Consider, for example, the number of books on the best-seller lists with "soul" in the title or recounting someone's spiritual journey, the number of popular movies featuring angels or dealing with the afterlife. There is a widespread interest in spirituality in our contemporary culture that often has no connection with traditional church life.

For mainline church leaders still struggling to understand this phenomenon, Wade Clark Roof's excellent study *A Generation of Seekers: The Spiritual Journeys of the Baby Boom Generation* remains must reading. "Baby boomers," he writes, "have found that they have to discover for themselves what gives their lives meaning, what values to live by. Not since the cataclysm of World War II have most of us been able simply to adopt the meanings and values handed down by our parents' religion, our ethnic heritage, our nationality. Rather, what really matters became a question of personal choice and experience."[1] And: "Boomers see religion in somewhat different ways than their parents did—with a greater concern for spiritual quest, for connectedness and unity, and for a vision that encompasses body and spirit, the material as well as the immaterial."[2]

There is an increasingly widespread distinction being made between being "spiritual" and being "religious." Those who say they are "spiritual" but not "religious" usually mean that they are genuinely concerned about their relationship with God, with the nurture of their inner life, with the well-being of their soul, but that they have little or no interest in traditional religious institutions, dogmas, or rituals. In my own experience, many who hold this perspective are those who have had bad experiences with the church—often either Roman Catholic or fundamentalist Protestant. They do not want their beliefs either spoon-fed or forced down their throats. These are people who want to think for themselves, to experience spiritual realities for themselves. They want nothing to do with "secondhand faith," which is how they would characterize the religion of the average churchgoer, whom they see as simply going through the motions of traditional religious rituals and organizational routines. For them spirituality has nothing to do with rummage sales, Christmas bazaars, committee busywork, and certainly not with the petty disputes in which they see active church people so often engaged.

It is awfully easy and tempting for church people to respond in kind. These spiritual seekers, we often charge, are only spiritual dabblers, jumping from fad to fad. So we dismiss them as New Age flakes, as hyperindividualists who understand little or nothing about the essentials of communal life and nurture, about the structure and accountability that traditional religious institutions provide. Congregations harboring such attitudes will, of course, have little or nothing to offer this generation of seekers. Congregations, on the other hand, who are willing to build bridges, who are ready to try to listen and learn can find themselves enriched in return.

This has been our experience at the Cathedral of Hope. In welcoming spiritually homeless strangers, our hospitality has been rewarded as we have found that we are welcoming angels in disguise. We have welcomed into our congregation a whole host of thoughtful, spiritually concerned, and serious persons who often come with many more questions than answers. In many instances what they have rejected are erroneous interpretations and distorted expressions of Christianity. They are eager and enthusiastic to learn about and to explore interpretations of Christian faith and life that make sense of it all in new ways that they have never before encountered.

Yes, these seekers are individualists. They want to think about and to experience God for themselves. But they are not necessarily lone wolves. Many of them are hungry for a spiritual community, a spiritual home base. They are delighted to discover and to connect with a church community that will accept them and take their questions and experiences seriously. They will embrace a community of pilgrims that will welcome them as fellow pilgrims. They will participate eagerly in give-and-take, mutually respectful explorations of spiritual and theological issues in which genuine differences of individual experience and insight are honored. In the process, they will challenge those of us in the church to rethink and reexamine our traditional beliefs and practices. All of this can serve to create a dynamic faith community characterized by truly exciting spiritual vitality and growth.

Matthew Fox—Evangelist
for a New Age of Seekers

In 1993 our membership growth committee took the risk of inviting to East Liberty Church a controversial theologian who is probably this current generation's very best builder of bridges between the Christian tradition and the spiritual sensibilities of our time. Matthew Fox—assiduous scholar, engaging teacher, and prolific author—is best known for his books *Original Blessing* and *The Coming of the Cosmic Christ.*[3] For many years he was a Roman Catholic priest and member of the Dominican order. In 1989, however, he was officially silenced by the Vatican and in 1993 he was dismissed by the Dominicans. Since then Fox has left the Roman Catholic Church and become an Episcopal priest.

What is it that seekers find attractive and many traditional Christians find objectionable in the writings of Matthew Fox? Fox aspires to being a both/and rather than an either/or thinker. I believe he is trying to offer balance to some of the old, one-sided emphases of Christian orthodoxy as he reads the tradition. I certainly do not always agree with Fox. I do not believe that he always succeeds in finding the balance he seeks, but I do believe that he aims to be true to the essence of the tradition as he understands it, even when he may radically reinterpret it. What follows is my own take on what I think Fox has to offer us. It's not necessarily the way Fox himself might formulate his own essential teaching, but here are some of the principal ingredients of his "Creation Spirituality" balancing act as I read him:

1. Balancing the traditional overemphasis on original sin with at least equal emphasis on original blessing—the essential goodness of our human nature as created in the image of God, an image that has not been, by any means, wholly defaced or destroyed by sin.

2. Balancing the traditional overemphasis on things "spiritual" with emphasis on the essential goodness of the physical, material world. The world of flesh and blood is God's creation. Our bodies are good; sex and other physical pleasures are, wisely used, wonderful blessings of a good God.

3. Balancing exclusivist Christian claims for Jesus Christ as the only way to God with the Cosmic Christ tradition that affirms a universal Christ presence in other faiths, cultures, and traditions.

4. Balancing passive, word-dominated worship with a whole-self worship that incorporates all the senses, movement, dance, celebration.

5. Balancing the anthropocentric, humans-subduing-and-dominating-the-earth tradition with emphasis on the earth as our mother. We have a God-given stewardship to protect and nurture the well-being of all creation.

6. Balancing the male-dominated Judeo-Christian traditions with rediscovery and reaffirmation of the feminine element in the divine (as found in the Wisdom/Sophia traditions of Proverbs and the Apocrypha, for example).

7. Balancing the priority given to the "great religions of the world" with respect and appreciation for the wisdom of primal, indigenous faiths such as those of the Native Americans and Celts who found the divine presence in all creation, in the daily and the ordinary.

8. Balancing Western Christianity's overemphasis on penal substitutionary atonement (God becoming human in Christ in order to take our place on the cross to suffer and die there for the forgiveness of our sins) with Eastern Christianity's emphasis on God becoming human in Christ in order to fully restore the divine image within us. In the Eastern tradition, the divine becomes human that the human might become divine.

9. Balancing the overemphasis on personal, individual sin and redemption with attention to the corporate and social nature of sin and salvation—understanding the sins we commit against nature and one another with our unjust and exploitative social, economic, and political systems and structures. The God of the Bible is a God of justice whose redemptive, delivering work is to overturn unjust systems, to liberate and deliver the poor, the oppressed, the exploited.

10. Balancing rationalistic, doctrinal approaches to faith with the rediscovery and reaffirmation of Christian mysticism—the *experience* of communion with God, of spiritual connectedness with all being.

11. Balancing an emphasis on a faithful way of life as entailing obedience to religious laws and authorities with an emphasis on nurturing and manifesting compassion, creativity, and a sense of connectedness with all being.

12. Balancing an emphasis on faithfulness as passivity, submission, and obedience with an emphasis on humans as co-creators with God. Uplifting the arts is a key way to celebrate and realize this divine potential within us.

An Invitation to Exploration

Despite the fact that I like to teach, believe that I have some gifts in this area, and enjoy free, wide-ranging discussions of theological issues and spiritual life concerns, no class I offered during my first five years at East Liberty Church seemed to create much interest among the old church constituency. At the start of my ministry, I took over leadership of an existing Sunday morning Bible study class for older adults. I did this for two years, then for a year I offered a new class on "Being Presbyterian." I followed that by leading a new Bible study for young adults for a couple of years. Not that numbers are everything, but none of these efforts attracted more than a dozen or so participants on a regular basis, sometimes considerably less.

After Matthew Fox's visit, it seemed we should do something to follow up on the large number of newcomers who had been attracted by his brief appearance. So, in January of 1994 we mailed out to all those who had attended the Fox workshop an invitation to participate in a Sunday morning class that would read and discuss his book *Creation Spirituality.*[4] From the start we dubbed it the Seekers Class. At our first meeting there were forty-five present—most of them new to our church! During the course of our initial discussion, about half of the newcomers identified themselves as former Roman Catholics and the other half as formerly affiliated with a fundamentalist Protestant church.

Also, in January and February of 1994, I offered a series of four sermons on "The New Age Challenge to Mainline Christianity." Individual sermons were entitled, "An Age of Spiritual Hunger," "A Hunger for Wholeness," "Many Paths, One Truth?" and "Is God within Us All?" At the outset, I recommended to the congregation for their reading *New Age Spirituality: An Assessment*, noting that it was published by our denominational press, Westminster John Knox, and edited by the director of our denominational unit on higher education, Duncan S. Ferguson.[5]

In accord with Ferguson's approach, I suggested that we should take a fair and open-minded approach to New Age faith expressions, just as I hoped we would with any other faith tradition: Buddhism, Hinduism, Islam, or other. Of course, I added, there are many nutty, off-track notions in some of the polymorphous expressions of New Age spirituality, notions incompatible with essential Christianity, which could also be said, of course, about certain expressions of Christianity itself. However, if we are willing and able to give thoughtful, honest, and fair attention to the essential themes of the New Age phenomenon, I believe we can learn a great deal about certain themes of the Christian tradition itself, such as mysticism, that we have long overlooked or suppressed. And we can learn a lot about what spiritually seeking people find missing in our mainline churches.

Wade Clark Roof has recently written words that could well serve as the charter of our Seekers Class:

> Religious communities should not act as if the larger spiritual climate does not exist—even within their own borders. . . . Religious leaders need to explore more deeply the resources within religious traditions and the affinities between these resources and people's spiritual questions and concerns. Traditional languages of faith and current rhetorics of spiritual searching already represent a gigantic cultural divide for many, especially the young. For religious communities, the creative and perhaps religiously responsible course would be to structure ways

in which believers and seekers might learn from one another and work
toward a shared vocabulary and practice.[6]

The Seekers Class is now six years old. Our numbers have waxed and waned
depending on the book that was the focus of our discussions, but the regular
class participation has held at between fifty and sixty people. Our study books
have ranged from *The Celestine Prophecy* by New Age author James Redfield
to *Jesus through the Centuries* by renowned Yale church historian Jaroslav
Pelikan. We have discussed *Reformed Spirituality* by Howard Rice and *The
Politics of Meaning* by Michael Lerner, *Care of the Soul* by Thomas Moore and
The Illustrated World's Religions by Huston Smith, *She Who Is* by feminist
theologian Elizabeth Johnson and *Living Buddha, Living Christ* by the famous
Vietnamese Buddhist monk Thich Nhat Hanh—to name only some.[7]
    In the Seekers Class I have felt that I was truly in my element, being where
I was meant to be, doing what I was meant to do. Moderating the weekly discussions of the Seekers, I was coming more and more to believe that this was
my special ministry, my special calling and gift from God. As the more evan-
gelically inclined used to phrase it, I do believe that God "laid on my heart a
burden" for this generation of seekers, though for me it is far more of a joy than
a burden. Much of my personal history had prepared me for this ministry. There
was my family history with a maternal grandfather who was a college professor and a freethinker, whose spirituality anticipated many of the New Age
themes. There was my mother, who was a devout and traditional yet open-
minded Christian believer who drew some of her inspiration from the Unity
School of Christianity. There was my older brother, who went into the ministry
eleven years ahead of me and challenged my youthful fundamentalism. There
were my many years of higher education, especially those seven years at
Harvard in the 1960s when the current seeker/new age gestalt had its birth. Last
but not least, there was my personal struggle with depression in the late '60s
and early '70s, which was, as much as anything I think, a grappling with the
new insights of a new generation with whom I was increasingly becoming a
spiritual cohort. The end result is that I thrive on dialogue with seekers. That is
my personal calling, my mission.
    Always in our Seekers Class we have striven to be open and respectful of
viewpoints that we may find strange or unacceptable, all the while encouraging
honest expression of our differences and disagreements with the authors and
with one another. We have also sought to honor our own Reformed Christian
tradition, to test it against other viewpoints and other viewpoints against it. The
hardest task for most of us, myself included, has been to keep a tolerant attitude
toward intolerant fundamentalism and exclusivism of any sort: Protestant,
Catholic, Jewish, Muslim, or other. But certain class members have made it
their mission to keep our feet to the fire, my own included, on this point as well.
    During the years of its life, the Seekers Class has become an important
"feeder" source for new friends, members, and leaders in our congregation.

With them, and a legion of supportive and understanding longtime members as well, we have been able to build a renewed, revitalized church. This class has been a major entry point for a whole host of able, personal growth-oriented, positive, dedicated, thoughtful "angels" who have found a congenial spiritual home at our Cathedral of Hope. And, for me and my wife, they have also proved to be our personal guardian angels, coming to our aid and comfort, our support and defense in the midst of a very difficult, painful time in our lives and in the life of our congregation.

9

A Tale of Two Churches

Our Other Church

How I dreaded those monthly meetings! Whenever I attended meetings of our board of trustees, I felt like I was in an entirely different church. What seemed like the best of times to most of us seemed like the worst of times to them. No one wanted to hear good news, even about their own church, maybe because they weren't so sure that it was still *their* church. Nit-picking and criticism were the rule. The prevailing mood was pessimistic. Very few trustees seemed able to see the big picture. We might be taking in more new members, but they weren't the right kind of people. We might be taking in more in contributions, but we were spending down the endowment—too much spent on advertising or programs or staffing.

Goodwill and a spirit of cooperation with other boards and committees of the church seemed pitifully elusive to our trustees. Meetings were filled with complaints about other church groups and programs. Some community group using the church gym had clogged up a toilet, so we should charge the repairs not to the trustees' property committee budget but to the session's community mission committee budget. After all, it was "those mission people" who were in charge of approving and overseeing building use by "those outside groups." Then the worship committee should be reprimanded because they had approved a staff request to spend a portion of the committee's year-end budget surplus to buy an electronic keyboard for use at the Service of Joy. And so on, and on, and on, month after month, year after year.

One of our trustees, who was especially practiced at micromanaging the church's daily operations, took it upon himself to install a lock on the door between the kitchen of the men's homeless shelter and the large adjacent room in which their Sunday worship service was held. This was apparently to make sure that the homeless men could not get access to the rest of the church building during the week, even though we had no indication that this was ever a problem. In fact, problems with vandalism or theft have been practically nonexistent. This is a sure sign, I believe, that the church is spared because our neighbors respect our outreach work in the community. Because the installation of that lock caused repeated problems getting the door unlocked for the shelter men to assemble for worship, I took it upon myself to have it removed.

The nadir with our trustees came after we suffered a dangerous near meltdown with our main church boiler. Fortunately, insurance covered most of the cost of constructing a new boiler. In the process, however, a handful of trustees decided to spend—over budget—a major amount to overhaul a second, backup boiler with which there was nothing apparently wrong. Contrary to proper Presbyterian procedure, this decision was never taken for approval to the session, the final authority in local church budget decision making. As the moderator of the session, I didn't even learn about it myself until it was a fait accompli!

One of my greatest frustrations was the extent to which misinformation kept circulating in the church, especially within the trustees, about church finance. While many perpetually insisted that we were spending down our endowment, that was simply not true. One trustee for two years circulated the rumor that the professional staff were getting larger percentage raises than the support staff. That too was untrue. Finally, in a joint meeting of the trustees and the session, I had to set the record straight.

I decided to prepare a simple quiz on basic East Liberty Church budget and finance facts and present it to the trustees, asking them to take it during one of their monthly meetings. The average grade was failing. (Our session, whom the trustees tended to scorn as fiscally irresponsible, had a better average grade!) That, however, did not deter the disinformation efforts. The prevailing attitude was "I know the truth, don't bother me with the facts." As one of our elders put it, these were folks who were "often wrong but never in doubt." Never in my life had I been in such a context where people would just keep on stating their views based on data that were blatantly false. Their version of the Bible apparently omitted the Ninth Commandment.

Chronic, Low-Intensity Conflict

Building and battling was how Nehemiah had to approach the rebuilding of Jerusalem's walls after the Jewish people returned home following their sixth century B.C. Babylonian captivity. Even as they worked on rebuilding the holy city, the workmen had to carry arms in order to protect themselves and their work from the enemies around them who were angered and threatened by the rebuilding of Jerusalem (Nehemiah 4). These, however, were *foreign* enemies. The opposition came from without, not from within; it did not pit Jew against Jew.

As a result of lessons learned the hard way in Vietnam's long civil war, the U.S. military introduced a new approach to counterinsurgency military action in Central America in the 1970s and '80s. This would be low-intensity warfare.

Its methods seem to describe the challenge we faced in our rebuilding campaign at our Cathedral of Hope. The notion was to beat the opposition at their own game. No big campaigns; just wear down the forces of change, bit by bit. Most of the action would be out of public view, out in the bush, up in the mountains. Most people in the society and the world at large would be unaware of the extent of it, unaware of the human cost, the pain, the atrocities. It would be a hidden war of attrition.

This is analogous to the tactics that many of us on the program staff often felt we were dealing with at ELPC—a quiet, persistent, virtually hidden campaign of attrition against change in the church. Working with certain committees, groups, and organizations in the church felt like walking through a minefield, being on guard for snipers and surprise attacks. Fortunately, as a staff we were pretty much in it together. We could sometimes handle it with humor, referring to the suspicion and hostility that we frequently encountered, for example, with a term coined by one of our staff members—"ankle biting."

Money wasn't the only subject of criticism and complaint, and our trustees were not the only ones to complain and criticize. The membership of the various longtime turf groups in the church tended to overlap and thus to foster and inculcate a similar story line about current church life within this "old turf network." Many individuals, of course, would be members of several different groups and organizations in the church. One and the same person could, for example, be a trustee, a choir member, a member of a church men's or women's group, a member of an adult Sunday school class, a member of the ushering team—each with its "fix" on church affairs. By this means certain points of view would be repeated, reinforced, and passed on to newcomers who might affiliate with such groups. Thus, to the degree that such groups shared the same basic viewpoints, it was easy for individuals who moved only or primarily within these select circles honestly to believe that their views were the majority views.

I had been warned at the start of my ministry about one of those old turf groups in particular, how members of that group, along with the choir and the music director (to whom I referred earlier), had been especially instrumental in the premature departure of my predecessor. It is my own inclination, however, and to a fault, according to my family, to give people the benefit of the doubt until I have my own reasons to believe otherwise. It was not until a number of years later, therefore, when I was at a social gathering of this particular group, that I looked around the room, and suddenly said to myself, "My God, here in one room are gathered virtually three-fourths of all those in the church who have had little to offer us but criticism and resistance!" Now it finally dawned on me. Much too late, I understood how and where certain newer members of the congregation were getting their rather quick indoctrination in a wide array of the same oppositional viewpoints held by many of the congregation's longtime insiders. Birds of a feather, whether new or old birds, flock together.

No wonder outsiders who had been invited to offer this particular group a program or presentation often came away saying that they would hope never to repeat the experience. A smug, know-it-all attitude seemed to prevail. A barrage of critical comments and questions awaited the outside presenter. Even members of our own Guatemalan Sister Parish task force, who had been asked to make a presentation to this group, left the meeting feeling demoralized, like their whole project had been met with nothing but suspicion and disapproval.

So it was that other members of the professional staff and I would sometimes feel worn down, worn-out, demoralized by trying to work in such contexts, contexts where we would repeatedly hear the following assertions, often utterly without foundation:

> We're spending down our endowment.
>
> We're spending too much on staff and programs.
>
> A church should not be seeking and receiving foundation grants.
>
> We're taking in too many new people who come in not knowing what they believe, that is, seekers.
>
> The new people we're taking in are not of solid "quality."
>
> We're only taking in transfers from other churches, not really attracting the unchurched.
>
> The variety of music being introduced is attracting the wrong kind of people.
>
> We shouldn't cater to people who don't like traditional Presbyterian worship and music. Those people should go elsewhere, to "their kind of church."
>
> The Taizé service is weird and un-Presbyterian. (Our music director dismissed it as a "seance.") No matter how many people like it, we shouldn't be doing it.
>
> We're losing our Presbyterian identity.
>
> The professional staff gives too much attention to newcomers and not enough to longtime members. They show favoritism to the black, the poor, the young.
>
> We're tapping new members for leadership positions too soon. They should be members for at least three years before being eligible for church office.
>
> The staff is fudging attendance figures, falsely inflating the numbers.
>
> The special events supported with costly advertising are bringing in lots of people who are not prospective members.
>
> The preaching is unbiblical, giving too much attention to current issues, current books, and motion pictures.

Fortunately for our morale, much of this internal negativity was counterbalanced by the good reports that kept coming back to us from throughout the neighborhood, the city, and the denomination—reports that we were accomplishing many good things at East Liberty Church, demonstrating what churches should be doing, providing good examples of how churches can and should adapt to changing times. We also knew that we had earned the trust and respect of some of Pittsburgh's most prominent philanthropic foundations, as evidenced in the significant grants we were receiving. As for the denomination at large, we felt tremendously affirmed by a feature story that appeared in the national *Presbyterian Survey* magazine in October 1994, "The Cathedral of Hope." Written by the same Pittsburgh "church critic" who had previously given us such a favorable review in the local media, this piece would, however, become yet another focus of criticism by our congregation's dissidents.[1]

Factors in Church Conflict

It should, of course, come as no surprise that change brings conflict, and the more extensive the change, the more extensive the conflict. Nancy Ammerman concludes her study of churches in changing communities with an observation that it is "absolutely clear that attempting significant changes will involve conflict, and congregations unwilling to engage in conflict will not change."[2] She also observes that the necessary change often must involve efforts to "dislodge old elites," and to develop structures of more broadly representative leadership, and that this will often lead to conflict.[3] Change that some welcome as good news is bad news to others. Jesus' gospel of reaching out with love to the outsiders was welcomed as good news by the outsiders, but rejected as bad news by the insiders. The hurt, hostile reaction of the older brother in the parable of the prodigal son makes this very point. So Jesus spoke of the difficulty of putting new wine in old wineskins, and of letting "the dead bury the dead." Obviously, he won few friends and followers among the Pharisees.

But can't change be gradual, incremental enough that everyone can be brought along in the process? Maybe. It sure sounds good, but it partly depends on how urgent is the perceived need for change that is pressing on us. Gradualism was the aim of the so-called Southern moderates in the civil rights conflicts of the 1960s. Those who felt that change was long overdue, however, saw the moderates as simply trying to buy more time for the status quo, to postpone even longer what had been already postponed far too long. As the civil rights leaders reminded us in the '60s and '70s and as gays and lesbians in our churches are reminding us again today, "Justice delayed is justice denied." In addition, of course, there is sometimes an opportunity to act that, if it is not seized, may never come again. A sense of urgency in a dying church that still has a sufficient critical mass of strength might enable that congregation to save the day only while the brief window of opportunity remains open.

In my first few years at East Liberty Presbyterian Church I was surprised that there was not more attrition of members. That typically occurs, of course, when there is a change of pastors, even more so when the new pastor initiates significant change. The answer to why we did not experience this attrition in my early years at the church lies in the particular local culture. Pittsburgh is the least mobile major city in the United States, meaning that the average resident is more likely to have lived here all his or her life than is the case in any other major American city. I found church members here more likely to be identified with their church through a history of family affiliation that stretched back for several generations. Extended families were more prevalent in this congregation than in any other I had ever served as pastor, and these families included family members and descendants of former pastors going back two generations. Even if they disliked intensely the new pastor and the changes he was bringing, they were not about to depart *their* church.

Other aspects of the local culture were involved. As I have noted earlier, Pittsburgh has much going for it, but there is a downside. Among Presbyterians nationwide there is an old saying that is meant to be taken both demographically and attitudinally: "Presbyterians are denser in Western Pennsylvania than anywhere else in the country." Perhaps it is the cultural residue of the long history of fighting and feuding among the Scottish and Scotch-Irish clans and among the various historic Presbyterian splinter groups. Perhaps it is partly left over from Pittsburgh's older history of intense labor-management conflict. In any event, there seems to be a real "culture of contention" here such as I have experienced nowhere else.

This is not just my outsider's viewpoint. It is a regional fact of life that is often lamented in the *Pittsburgh Post-Gazette*, now the city's single major daily newspaper. In editorials, opinion columns, and special series on the region's future, there is frequent and honest self-examination of the attitude problem here: negativism, factionalism, parochialism, resentment toward new people and new ideas. A September 1998 editorial warned of a "stultifying atmosphere in which new and creative ideas are unable to flourish." Recently there appeared in the *Post-Gazette* a local columnist's comments on the sad fact that members of the Pittsburgh Board of Education had just taken ten votes before they were able to elect one of their number as president. The column is replete with references to "perpetual squabbling," "petty turf wars," "fractious behavior," and "political infighting." In the fall of 1995, when my pastoral leadership at East Liberty Church was on the line, I heard a statement from a network TV sports commentator that turned on a lightbulb for me. "It's hard to be a quarterback in Pittsburgh," he said. "They'll boo you even when you're winning." It was true. I had witnessed it myself at the Three Rivers Stadium . . . and at the Cathedral of Hope.

In my church and community experiences elsewhere, after a couple of conflicting parties had butted heads for a while, one or both would eventually come to the conclusion that the process was pointless and self-defeating. So they would give up and go away. Not so here. Head butting seemed almost a way of life for some—as if they thrived on it, as if they knew no other way. One especially troublesome church member as much as admitted to me that she enjoyed mixing it up in a good church fight.

The "terrible trio" in our choir—three men who were among the most entrenched of our members in their resistance to change, not only musical change, but just about any sort of change—provide another interesting case study. These three were implacable opponents, first of mine, then later of our new music director as well. In this they were united. In other respects, however, they were sometimes literally at one another's throats. Individual A and individual B were related by marriage, but A was not on speaking terms with B. Individual C's wife could not stand A, who was her supervisor at work, so A and C were not on good terms either. In fact, one Sunday A and C were about to come to blows in the choir robing room until B intervened to physically separate them. All three, by the way, are professionals. One was an elder, one a trustee.

I have seen this sort of dynamic at work here not only in our congregation but also in neighboring congregations, in Pittsburgh Presbytery, and in our community organizations. I have heard about it from leaders of some of the city's most prominent cultural organizations, about how they initially had to battle entrenched, self-perpetuating, old guard elites who resisted change and held on to long-outdated attitudes and methods. In one case, I am told, getting rid of a particularly troublesome, self-perpetuating women's auxiliary in one of these organizations finally came down to an executive decision to change the locks on their office door!

Conflict is especially difficult for churches. After all, we are supposed to follow Jesus' commands to love and forgive one another, to give one another the benefit of the doubt, and not to question one another's motives. The result often is that those who are unafraid of conflict—who are, in fact, disposed to create it and stir it up—will be given the advantage by the acquiescence of a more timid majority who want to avoid unpleasantness. As Dr. James Forbes, pastor of the Riverside Church in New York City, recently put it to me, "Liberal Christians do not make good fighters. They are too tolerant, have too much goodwill." A relatively few dissidents, therefore, with loud and negative voices, with active telephone and e-mail networks, can carry a weight and pack a punch far in excess of their numbers. Those with negative attitudes often seem to work up an emotional head of steam that more positive-minded individuals cannot muster. So the rest of us too often play the role of enablers. We concede to the troublesome few and allow them to exercise their "sour power" over us and over our congregations.

As with many congregations, this enabling of chronically difficult people— on the staff, in the lay leadership, and in the congregation at large—was also a part of East Liberty's history and culture. (Years before my arrival, an unpopular church business manager was finally "terminated" when a disgruntled employee shot him to death in the church office during a staff Christmas party!) Certain members had been allowed to claim inordinate amounts of the pastor's and the session's time and attention with their endless series of complaints and grievances. With the most blatant case that had gone on for years and years, the session finally declared in the early '90s that they would entertain no more communications from this particular individual. It worked! No more was heard from that person, someone who had succeeded in getting so much negative attention over such a long time.

In another case, the chairperson of session's personnel committee and the clerk of session were willing to sit down with our business administrator and me to deal with a member of our board of trustees, the one previously mentioned who was so adept at trying to micromanage daily operations. We successfully intervened to stop the day-to-day work interruptions and personal misery that this individual's actions were causing for our business administrator, who had been hired to do the job without having someone constantly looking over his shoulder and making inordinate demands for time and information.

These hard psychosocial, political realities in congregational life are only lately beginning to be acknowledged in the church at large. In recent years books have been written and workshops offered on "coping with difficult people." M. Scott Peck pushed the focus beyond merely difficult people in his *People of the Lie*. I had left that book unread on my study shelves for some years until I found myself dealing with a couple (white, upper-middle-class professionals who were solid members of one of the congregation's old turf in-groups) who were systematically abusing their children. In this somewhat frightening book, I found Peck warning that because such people "tend to gravitate toward piety for the disguise and concealment it can afford them . . . one of the places evil people are most likely to be found is within the church."[4] Much more recently, Lloyd Rediger's popular book *Clergy Killers* is finally bringing the topic of church hostility and destructiveness the attention it deserves.[5]

One of the best and most concise statements of this problem that I have come across is an article, "When Congregations Are Stuck" by Peter L. Steinke, author of *Healthy Congregations: A Systems Approach.*[6] Steinke puts his finger precisely and firmly on the problem that troubles many of our declining congregations: a close-knit group of longtime members in positions of power who are anxious and threatened by any changes that might shake up their control and their comfort with things as they are and who are allowed to intimidate those who favor change. With a wonderfully revealing phrase with multiple meanings—emotional, spiritual, developmental, sociological, organizational—Steinke says that these are people who are often "stuck together." "The pressure to be a member of the club who does not rock the boat will override any attempt to change and risk tilting the system. And clergy who are unaware of the togetherness forces will find themselves caught in the system's emotional buzz-saw."[7]

People of goodwill want to avoid conflict and pain, so they acquiesce or fade away. Pain, however, as Steinke notes, may be the necessary prelude to significant and long-overdue change. The essential ingredients are pain plus highly motivated leaders willing to face up to it and endure it for the sake of moving the congregation forward toward the realization of its full potential.

There *are* troubled individuals and dysfunctional groups in the church just as there are elsewhere in society. There *are* persons who carry their dysfunctional family dynamics over into the church family. There *are* people who project onto others and act out their own inner conflicts within the group. There *are* those in our pews, on our boards and committees, who are abusive to their children, their spouses, and their pastors. There *are* those who, the sad truth to tell, will rise to the occasion only when they smell conflict brewing, only when they get "a whiff of blood." There *are* those who are hopelessly, compulsively oppositional personalities. As Steinke so rightly urges, congregations and denominations need methods, mechanisms, and specially trained leadership that can recognize these hard realities and stand ready and willing to deal with them. Otherwise, the often easier but frequently unjust solution will be perpetuated, making the pastor the sacrificial lamb when the conflict gets intolerable.

One of my problems with much of the conflict resolution and intervention procedures applied in our churches is the failure to deal with the long-standing realities of dysfunctional personalities and dysfunctional group dynamics in congregations. This is, of course, a difficult and tricky challenge. What denominational representative or outside consultant wants to be responsible for alienating a significant bloc of any congregation? Often it's much simpler and less time-consuming simply to yank the pastor. But any course of action is going to result in the loss of some members, so why not bite the bullet, name the demons, and then take a course of action that furthers the long-term health and growth of a congregation?

Why Can't We All Just Get Along?

One of the most effective illustrations of a point that I have ever witnessed was in a workshop led by Stephen Covey, author of *The Seven Habits of Highly Effective People*.[8] There must have been three to four hundred people present, seated at round tables in a large ballroom at Pittsburgh's Convention Center. First Covey asked us all to close our eyes. "Now," he said, "point toward north." Next he told us to keep pointing, to open our eyes, and to look around. Hands were outstretched everywhere, pointing in all conceivable directions. Covey's final instruction was to stand, join hands with others at our table, and all move together toward north! It was, of course, impossible since we didn't agree about which way was north. The point? Without organizational mission and vision statements as a basis for agreement about the direction in which we are trying to move forward together, there is only confusion, chaos, and conflict.

There is, of course, nothing inherently wrong with differences of opinion and dissenting views about the best direction in which a group or organization ought to be moving. In democratic societies, in fact, we tend to consider the absence of differing views more of a problem, symptomatic of oppressive leadership and the suppression of freedom of thought and expression. We believe that a free and open give-and-take of opinions will tend to bring us closer to the truth, closer to solutions that will meet a wider range of needs in the community. By and large, this is certainly true when there is a prevailing respect for diversity of opinions and of needs. The open system works best when there is a general willingness to "agree to disagree agreeably," to quote the motto of a predecessor of mine in a previous pastorate (who said that he picked it up from a rabbi). The best way to get our differing views out on the table for discussion and then come to some resolution about where we were headed, it seemed to me, was to initiate a comprehensive, congregational strategic planning process. In early 1992, therefore, I made this recommendation to our session, which responded by authorizing the appointment of a representative strategic planning committee. The result was a committee truly representative of our congregation in viewpoints, race, gender, age, social class, and length of membership.

My hopes were very high that the planning process would lead us, if not to consensus about the church's plans and priorities, at least to agreement among such a solid majority that we could name our identity as a congregation and set our directions for the future. Much would still depend, of course, on the disposition of whatever minority might remain once our plan was formulated. When all was said and done, would those who still wanted us to go in a different direction be willing to disagree agreeably, to let the majority move on toward what most of us would identify as our congregation's north star?

10

The Best-Laid Plans

Getting at "the Vision Thing"

President George Bush admitted to some puzzlement about what he referred to as "the vision thing." He was criticized for not being able to articulate any grand vision for the future of the country. He seemed unable to understand what people were looking for and how to help them find it. He seemed to understand the presidency more as a maintenance operation.

How do nations, groups, organizations, congregations derive their vision, their sense of common purpose, their direction into the future? What compass tells them which way is north? Does it come from visionary leaders, from the top down? Does it come from the people themselves, from the bottom up? Is it a combination of both?

It helps, I believe, to understand how individuals come by their own personal sense of purpose, their mission, their calling. Personal history is an important ingredient. How have we been shaped by our family, our unique experiences, the regional and cultural milieu in which we have come to maturity? Life history, of course, need not be completely determinative. Sometimes God calls us to change, to learn and grow in significant new ways. Sometimes we have transforming experiences or make life-changing decisions that take us in new directions radically different from those that our past alone might have predicted.

Our own unique gifts and talents, our natural interests and inclinations, our educational opportunities and personal beliefs and values also give us powerful pointers into the future. We are motivated to make the most of what we have been given, to live a life that fulfills our God-given potential and that is consistent with our highest values and our best selves. We need also, of course, to be mindful of what it is we most enjoy doing.

Social confirmation is important. What do friends, family, coworkers tell us about what we do well, about when we are at our best and when we truly shine?

What builds our self-esteem, what affords us recognition and rewards us with a sense of making a significant contribution to the welfare of others, to the common good? How do our own gifts and abilities, interests and inclinations, values and convictions correspond to the needs and opportunities of our time and place?

All these same factors, I believe, will go into a congregation's efforts to define its mission and vision, to chart its course into the future. There will be theological input. What are our core beliefs and values? There will be input from the congregation's history. Who have we been and what have we done in the past? There will be an assessment of the church's resources, its strengths and abilities. There will be an analysis of its unique context, its neighborhood or larger community. What is it that the people around us want and need from us that we have to offer? How has our larger context changed? What do our beliefs and values lead us to keep on doing or to start doing? What do we do well and feel rewarded in doing? What do we not do so well that we might learn to do better? What is not being offered by other congregations or agencies that our congregation might be able to provide? How do we need to change in order to be responsive to human need, to do what God is calling us to do here and now?

All of this exploration, I believe, best takes place through an open-ended dialogical process that is a mix of both top-down and bottom-up input. Visionary leaders are always needed. At the same time, our scriptures affirm that all God's people are granted the Holy Spirit's gift of seeing visions and dreaming dreams: the young and the old, women and men, those at the top and those at the bottom of the social ladder (Acts 2:17–18). A steering and guiding mechanism is needed, however, so that the process is not chaotic, is given shape and form. A filtering process is required so that raw input is assessed, evaluated, and refined. This is where the role of a planning committee comes in. The congregation's governing body, of course, will also have a key role in receiving, revising, and acting upon recommendations from the planning committee.

The particular advantage of professional leadership in the planning process should be an ability to stand with one foot in and one foot out of the local congregation. Pastors should bring to the process a vision that is rooted in the local church yet broadened by experience and knowledge of congregations elsewhere, by reading and travel and continuing education exposures that bring awareness of current practices and trends, by deeper and broader biblical and theological understanding, and by the benefit of giving their full-time attention to the very issues which the planning process concerns.

Much of the above accounts for the fact that I waited over three years before initiating a comprehensive, broad-based planning effort at East Liberty Presbyterian Church. It seemed important first to offer the congregation some exposure to new ideas and new possibilities, to broaden the horizons of imagination before beginning officially to envision our future. Also, I wanted enough time to pass so that by the time we started planning we could have recruited a sufficient cadre of new members to provide a goodly infusion of new blood, new input into our planning process.

Even before our comprehensive planning process got under way, however, we had good direction from the following sources:

> The congregational survey undertaken by the pastoral search committee during the interim period between senior pastors.
>
> An informal survey I had conducted, even before arriving on the scene, by asking the church office to mail to all members a simple questionnaire with only two questions: (1) What do you believe are the strengths of ELPC; (2) Where do you think ELPC has room for improvement?
>
> A good sense of where the congregation was coming from theologically, socially, and politically, which was basically a moderate, middle-of-the-road Presbyterianism.
>
> Congregational input from our "Marketing the Church" workshop in early 1989.
>
> The intermediate range plan that I drafted after one year, a plan that was then discussed and approved by the church officers.

How We Did It

When we got under way in early 1992, we had a strategic planning committee that was very broadly representative in terms of male and female, younger and older members, whites and blacks, longtime and newer members, theological liberals, moderates and conservatives. From the start, we were blessed to have as our chairperson an exceedingly able, open-minded, well-respected, life-long member of the congregation who had held many leadership positions in the church and was a partner in one of the city's top law firms. One member of the committee, the director of public relations at a major corporation and one of our newer members, was especially good at writing for the general public and provided immense help in drafting our documents. Another committee member, a medical doctor and vice-president of a major Pittsburgh hospital and a newer member, was a top-notch process person who proved invaluable in facilitating the congregational sessions that, later in the process, would prove very effective in gathering input from across our entire membership.

The planning committee's first efforts focused on formulating draft statements of our mission and vision, our core values, our priorities, and our "callings" as a congregation. These were finished by the early fall of 1992 and presented to the session for discussion. The session made some relatively minor revisions that were incorporated into the final documents approved that December. The combined mission and vision statement was based on our "Reaching Up, Reaching Out, Reaching You" tag line, which had come out of our early 1989 congregational workshop on "Marketing the Church." It read as follows:

Our Mission and Vision Statement

REACHING UP to God with many voices and various styles	REACHING OUT to neighbors near and far with a witness of hope	REACHING YOU unique and precious in God's sight and in ours
• celebrating with joyful, spirit-filled praise God's redeeming love in Christ • seeking God's gracious plan for our congregation and for each of us • offering ourselves in faithful and loving service to God	• serving God by serving the human need in our congregation, community, and world • affirming by all we do our commitment to peace, justice, and human dignity for all people • inviting all to join our diverse, inclusive family of faith • utilizing in mission our unique combination of location and facilities, people and material resources	• embracing your individuality and personal spiritual journey • responding compassionately to your needs • nurturing a spirit that is loving, forgiving, and caring • developing our full, God-given potential as we learn and grow together

Obviously, the statement reflects a strong affirmation of the congregation's inclusivity and diversity as key to our identity, a gift and source of strength to be celebrated and nurtured. A diversity of individual spiritual paths and journeys is affirmed, as are various styles of worship. The statement also communicates a commitment to balance between the spiritual and the missional dimensions of our life together, between worship and prayer on the one hand and the active pursuit of peace and justice on the other hand. Commitment to our local neighborhood and its needs is balanced with world vision and concern.

Other elements of the plan's initial pieces underscored a strong commitment to comprehensive, holistic growth—growth in spirituality and discipleship, growth in mission outreach and in numbers of new members recruited. The core values included a commitment to continue building "a richly diverse faith community which witnesses to our oneness in Christ across all boundaries of race, social class, culture, gender, and lifestyle." After some brief discussion as to whether or not we should make an explicit affirmation to welcome people without regard to their sexual orientation, the committee concluded that the reference to "lifestyle" was sufficient to cover this point. Personally, I was not altogether satisfied with this approach because sexual orientation is not, in my estimation, a lifestyle choice, but I decided at that point not to make an issue of it. Besides, being explicit on this issue might just generate unproductive conflict at that point in the church's development.

During 1993 the planning committee worked with the congregation to develop programmatic proposals and priorities for the church. Three opportunities, including one full-day retreat, were offered and all members and friends of the church were invited. A democratic process called Storyboarding was used both to stimulate imagination and brainstorming and to reduce the number of proposals put forward to a manageable number. By this method sixty-seven program proposals were developed, each one listed under one or another of twelve major "Callings of the Congregation" that had been identified by the planning committee and approved by the session. These twelve callings included such primary, overarching goals as: "To share the love of Christ and to increase our numbers by attracting new members and friends who are not presently part of a Christian community" and "To develop and pursue a sound financial plan to serve our mission and vision."

Examples of the sixty-seven program proposals identified include:

> Conduct an ongoing program of inviting well-known speakers, preachers, and workshop leaders who will offer a special appeal to the unchurched.
>
> Be intentionally multicultural in our worship, music, and arts planning, being especially inclusive of the African American heritage.
>
> Encourage and enable each member and friend to participate in at least one aspect of mission work, helping individuals to identify their calling and match their talents and interests with opportunities at hand.
>
> Provide one-on-one spiritual companioning and training in prayer, meditation, and spiritual companioning to our members and friends.

I should also note that our entire planning process followed what is sometimes called the plan-and-do approach; that is, we did not wait until the end of the planning process to implement some of the good ideas that arose as we were planning. In fact, it sometimes seemed that the planning process was struggling to keep up with many of the experiments and innovations we were already developing.

Resolving Thorny Issues?

It had long been my hope that the development of a comprehensive plan would help us by resolving some of the conflicted points that kept bogging us down in endless, unproductive dispute and disagreement. Among these issues were the variety of our worship and music styles, the endowment spending patterns, professional staffing design and program costs, tensions between facilities expenditures on the one hand and spending for mission and ministry on the other, and organizational conflicts and confusions between session and the trustees.

I was delighted with our plan on each of these points. The strong affirmation of worship and music diversity has already been noted. In addition, there were clear and forthright statements in the plan that all our priorities and decisions were to be ministry and mission driven. There was a bold, up-front commitment to "approach all our church planning with our uppermost priority being to share God's love in Christ with one another and with others outside our congregation, keeping in mind the needs and interests of those without a church home as we shape our present and future programming, staffing, facilities, and budgeting plans."

Our program goals called on us to "develop a five-year financial plan and allocate financial resources primarily on the basis of our program goals and priorities." The financial guidelines of the five-year plan that was developed and approved noted that, notwithstanding the fact that there were those in the congregation "who have expressed the concern that our financial picture is bleak . . . , the endowment today is *11 percent bigger in real dollars* than it was at the beginning of the '80s." The plan went on to affirm that the need "to *invest in the future*" is "*not only prudent but absolutely necessary to assure the continued life and vitality of this congregation.*" Current program needs, the church's well-being, and endowment growth over the past fifteen years, the document stated, "both justify and require withdrawals from the endowment significantly in excess of the total return." The plan called for "reasonable, prudent risk taking in our financial decisions as an expression of faith in our congregation's future." The budgeting guidelines, therefore, allowed for the possibility that over the five-year period from 1995 through 1999 the real dollar value of the endowment might be drawn down by as much as 15 percent of its value as of midyear 1993.

The plan's section on "Church Organizational Structure" called for the revision of our outdated congregational bylaws and for the merger of the trustees and the session into one body. The planning committee felt so strongly about this latter point, in fact, that even before the whole plan was completed they took to session in 1993 a recommendation to effect a merger of these two boards. The session agreed and called for a special congregational meeting in June of 1993 to act upon the matter. The trustees were divided among themselves, though a majority of them probably opposed it. Officially, they took no action on the matter. The mainly longtime church members who opposed the merger spoke of the need for "a balance of power" in church governance. They were apparently unaware that their argument reflected a serious misinterpretation of the relationship of the two boards in our Presbyterian *Book of Order*. A separate board of trustees may exist only as a body that is clearly subordinate in all matters to the session. Opponents also insinuated that approving the merger would be handing over too much power to the pastor, who, according to Presbyterian polity, must act as moderator of the session and would, of necessity, be the moderator of a merged board.

The congregational vote on the merger fell three votes short of the two-thirds majority needed for approval, a major disappointment. The planning committee, which would continue its work for another year, decided not to press the board merger issue again during its remaining tenure.

I believe two paragraphs from our plan's section on church organization deserve special attention here because they speak to issues that are of major significance for mainline church vitality now and in the future. There are pivotal concerns here for all churches that have a tradition of involving lay people in the work of the church principally through membership on boards and committees:

> We are concerned that our organizational structure causes excessive time to be spent on organizational matters—business meetings, structural matters, process issues—with the result that many church leaders, lay and staff alike, have too little time to spend on our primary focus: study, worship, and service. A further result is that many decisions take far longer than good management practices dictate and our fast-paced world permits. We have heard time and again, both from within our committee and from all constituencies within the church, that our members, particularly our leaders, would like to spend a greater percentage of their time in study, worship, and service and less time in meetings.

> We suggest attempts be made to meet this concern by considering both revisions to church organizational structure and to the approach to actual board and committee functioning whereby our boards and committees focus, first, on planning and visioning and, then, on reviewing and evaluation, leaving the day-to-day managing of activities to staff and individual lay leaders charged with implementation responsibility. This does not mean less lay leadership involvement. It means more involvement in the form of serving and doing and less in the form of meeting attendance.

The chairperson of our planning committee, who was the author of these two paragraphs, had for many years expressed his opinion that "we Presbyterians have a tendency to get entangled in our procedural underwear." An elder in one of my previous congregations had characterized Presbyterian polity as a game of "Mother, may I?" Sad to say, after our June 1993 congregational meeting, we were still stuck with what I called a "Rube Goldberg organizational design."

11

Facing the Music

Out of Tune

Our longtime music director retired in the summer of 1993. Though he had held a full-time position and had the help of a part-time assistant, what we had to show for it in the end was basically a performance quality organist and the fine adult chancel choir that he directed from the organ bench. There were by then no other choirs or musical organizations in the church for children, youth, or adults, no bell choirs or instrumental ensembles.

Most likely he could have made more than this happen in a traditional suburban church, but the unique challenge of trying to relate to a culturally diverse inner-city population was apparently too great. When our senior high bell choir fell by the way, I encouraged the formation of a combined youth and adult bell choir, if we could not muster enough of either age group alone. Or how about trying to form a combined bell choir from the youth of several different neighboring congregations? There was always some reason this or that wouldn't work in our situation. This "can't do" attitude was not so surprising, however, once you had heard one of his choice quotes from George Bernard Shaw. Speaking of the volunteer instrumentalists who were playing for our Taizé service, he came forth at one of our staff meetings with, "Hell is full of amateur musicians." His particular complaint at that point was that their instruments were out of tune. To myself I thought, "How much worse it is when our spirits are out of tune." Anyway, you must admit that it would indeed be difficult to organize a broadly participatory music ministry on the basis of a motto such as Shaw's!

I would characterize the music of our Sunday morning 11:00 A.M. service as "museum quality," polished, technically correct, and cold. There were some notable exceptions, but typically it felt like a performance "under glass," impressive but distant, lacking soul. I knew exactly what Thomas Moore meant when I read his reflections about narcissistic cultural products in his *Care of the*

Soul: works of art that are contained, "marble-like" and "self-absorbed," yet subtly communicate a lack of self-confidence by calling too much attention to themselves.[1] When "the fine arts are elevated and set apart from life," he writes, they become "too precious and therefore irrelevant."[2]

Moore deserves more attention on the subject of art, religion, and soul:

> When we leave art only to the accomplished painter and the museum, instead of fostering our own artful sensibilities through them, then our lives lose opportunities for soul. The same is true when we leave religion to church on the weekend. Then religion remains on the periphery of life, even if it is an exalted periphery, and life loses opportunity for soul. Fine art, like formal religion, is at times quite lofty, while soul in any context is lower case, ordinary, daily, familial and communal, felt, intimate, attached, engaged, involved, affected, ruminating, stirred and poetic.[3]

As they faced one another across the extraordinarily wide expanse of our divided chancel with its floor of highly polished Italian marble, our choir members were literally singing to themselves. Acoustical problems were compounded by the fact that sound-absorbing acoustical tile had been installed in the sanctuary vault when the church was constructed. The choir thus sounded faint and far away and congregational singing was abysmal in that great, cavernous, dead space. Yet all efforts to adjust for these difficulties, such as having the choir sing from the chancel steps, or using sound amplification, or having a cantor to lead and support congregational singing, were adamantly resisted as aesthetically incorrect.

Over a period of years these attitudes had been pretty thoroughly inculcated within at least two-thirds of the choir, a mix of paid and volunteer singers. When I recruited our seminary intern and my wife to sing "Eat This Bread, Drink This Cup" to guitar accompaniment as people were receiving the sacrament during a Communion service, Jan heard many favorable comments afterward from members of the congregation. She also, however, overheard snide comments from choir members about that "Puff the Magic Dragon" piece. Jan, bless her heart, stuck it out singing in the chancel choir during our first four years at East Liberty Church. For a sensitive, caring soul it exacted a price, but I'm grateful that she persevered as long as she did because her presence surely helped to prevent much worse things from being more openly expressed.

On Pentecost Sunday in 1992, we premiered our new church video at the 11:00 A.M. service. The plan was for the choir to come down from the chancel at that point to sit in the front pews in order to view the video and then to join the congregation in a "come forward" (rather than seated in the pews) Holy Communion. Instead, half the choir and the music director simply left the church at that point. Why? Several reasons probably: objections to the video being shown in the service, opposition to a "coming forward" Communion, offended feelings about the choir being asked to leave the chancel and sit among the congregation with ordinary worshipers. Incredibly, some of the most arrogant attitudes were often displayed by paid singers, some of whom were not even members of the church. That was the day Jan decided, for the sake of her own spiritual and emotional well-being, she had to quit the choir.

Sing to the Lord a New Song

About a year before our music director's retirement date, a search committee was appointed to find his replacement. The committee was co-chaired by two longtime church members. Both of them were also choir members, frequent church officeholders, and one of them was also a member of the strategic planning committee. Because they were open-minded people and sensitive both to the importance of tradition and to the need for change, they gave us a wonderful combination of leadership qualities for this crucial undertaking.

The search committee's first effort was to formulate a statement of philosophy and goals for a ministry of music and the arts. It quickly became clear that the task was not to find a "replacement" for the kind of leadership we had in the past. With the able facilitation of that same member of the strategic planning committee who proved so helpful in enabling congregational participation in shaping our comprehensive church plan, the search committee began to outline a whole new vision of ministry in music and the arts. Their work was eventually approved by session and incorporated into the church strategic plan. It boldly charted a brand-new course:

Music and Arts Program Goals

The purpose of the music and arts program is to glorify God, both in our church and in the community. The program will:

> involve the whole person, body, mind, and spirit in worship and fellowship;
> promote participation in worship, celebration, and meditation;
> welcome God's inspiration and seek to offer God our best;
> be responsive to our congregation's diverse spiritual needs and cultural tastes;
> be intergenerational, multicultural, and relevant to the local community;
> be a means of evangelism, outreach, and church growth;
> create a community from the diversity of our congregation;
> provide opportunity for each person to express his or her personality and spirituality;
> enhance, vitalize, and integrate the worship services;
> promote widespread involvement in the music and arts program.

The statement of "Music and Arts Staffing Requirements" that accompanied this statement of program goals called for developing a music and arts staff that could work as team players with one another and with the entire church staff. We would seek a director of music and the arts possessing the organizational and administrative skills to develop and coordinate a diverse program that would include various choral and instrumental groups as well as incorporating other arts such as drama, dance, visual arts, and creative writing. We would seek a director who could instruct and inspire congregational participation; work skillfully with diverse cultural groups of all ages; draw from diverse musical traditions such as African American, classical, and popular; and approach his or her work as a committed, caring Christian. A tall order, indeed, but finally a new day was dawning!

These two statements of program goals and staffing requirements were presented to and discussed with our chancel choir soon after the music director's retirement, but another year would elapse before a new person was in place in the fall of 1994. In the meantime, we would employ a part-time interim organist and a part-time interim choral director.

Still Out of Tune

We were blessed to find an excellent interim choral director who was on the music faculty at the University of Pittsburgh and director of the school's esteemed Heinz Chapel choir. He was a classically trained musician with broad musical tastes and abilities. He was also a fine colleague—cooperative, flexible, open-minded, possessed of a gentle, caring spirit—and fit in beautifully with the church's ministry and program staff. We hoped he would be with us until our new permanent person was found, but it was not to be.

Our new interim director soon had our choir singing from the chancel steps, singing to the congregation rather than to themselves from their pew stalls. His repertoire included many popular spirituals that were a big hit with the congregation, black and white alike. The resistance from certain choir members, however, proved too much for him, too much hostility, rudeness, even outright defiance. Four months were all he could take. He left us, still without a permanent music director, at the end of 1993. The choir had been well trained. The session goals meant nothing. The congregation's preferences didn't matter. The choir alone knew what was best for us musically.

At a session meeting in late 1993, one of our African American elders remarked how wonderful the choral music had been the past several months under our interim's leadership, especially the spirituals. Others, both black and white, joined in with enthusiastic agreement. Then a white woman married to a black man, both of them professional musicians with one of the city's premiere ensembles, had the last word. "Well," she huffed, drawing herself up, "as my husband says, 'I don't need to be sung down to!' " End of discussion. Clearly the narcissistic perspective prevailed in such minds: It doesn't matter what others prefer, the point is to satisfy *me*.

Her husband was a longtime member of our worship and music committee who, having heard in advance of my plan to have our seminary intern and my wife play and sing their so-called "Puff the Magic Dragon" piece, had demanded to know why on earth we were planning to have a guitar at 11:00 A.M. worship. I suppose it shouldn't have surprised me, but it did—the vehement resistance to musical inclusivity that we encountered from a small but vocal number of archconservative African American members, many of them in our choir, many of them long-term officeholders in the church.

One of this cadre (call him "Clarence") was so conservative that other conservatives in the congregation described him as "somewhere to the right of Attila the Hun." Clarence did not hide his opinion that, as far as any kind of music other than classical was concerned, the church should not be catering to *those kinds* of people who would like *that kind* of music. He was one of those who thought that, in spite of its growing popularity, we should not be offering our weekly Taizé service. Clarence and his cohorts were steadfastly opposed to music from the African American church tradition, especially gospel music that was anathema to them. These were middle- to upper-middle-class folks who had joined the congregation many years before, when it was still overwhelmingly white and still had some cachet as an upper status church. I could only conclude that they had personally invested a great deal over many years in putting as much distance as they could between themselves and their own cultural heritage, which they looked down upon as unworthy and inferior. It was a sad conclusion, but it helped me understand and muster a bit of compassion for Clarence and others like him who sometimes seemed filled with such bitterness, anger, and scorn.

My own musical tastes were no secret. I was brought up to love and appreciate classical music. Most of the recordings in our home collection when I was growing up were classical. I sang and played classical music in my junior and high school chorus and band. Today, though I do enjoy a wide variety of music, I still listen mainly to classical and jazz. But I try to resist my own elitist tendencies. I try to be open and inclusive. In the final analysis, as far as the outreach of the church is concerned, what matters most is not what I like. What matters most is what will reach the people we need to reach, what will speak to them and meet their needs. That's why, from the pulpit, I recommended Whoopi Goldberg's movie *Sister Act* as a top-notch example of how churches need to change to meet the needs of their changing contexts. To the opponents of musical change and adaptation in our choir and congregation that could only mean that, in my heart of hearts, I really hated classical music. For them, it seemed, it was either/or. There could be no compromise, no mix, no blend of musical cultures.

This account may seem exaggerated, but I assure you it is not. The phenomenon is not unknown in many other mainline churches across the country, accounting for the little joke that has made the ministerial rounds in recent years: "What's the difference between a terrorist and a classically trained church musician? You can negotiate with a terrorist!" Thus Lyle Schaller's observation that in many a church the music department is also known as "the war department."

But What Do People Want?

What did our congregation as a whole think about all this? In the spring of 1994 we conducted a comprehensive churchwide survey of worship and music opinions and preferences in the congregation. We color-coded the questionnaires so that we could compare results obtained from the different worship services and from the choir as well. The choir, however, derailed their part of the process, insisting that they must use the same questionnaires as other 11:00 A.M. worshipers. They apparently did not want their opinions distinguished from and compared with those of the worshiping congregation as a whole, being rightly fearful, I suspect, that the contrast would be too revealing.

The results, nevertheless, *were* revealing. As far as musical tastes were concerned, worshipers at the 11:00 A.M. service expressed a liking for classical, gospel, spirituals, Taizé, contemporary praise songs, and jazz. The most frequently registered dislikes were for jazz, Taizé, praise, and folk music, yet all these negative responses were relatively small percentages of the total: 10 percent to 15 percent. Over 71 percent of the respondents favored a mix of musical styles in worship, while 54 percent felt that the worship was not yet offering as much musical variety as they preferred. By popular electoral standards, these returns would represent a landslide and a mandate for diversity.

In response to a question concerning the mix of formality and informality in the service, 60 percent preferred either a balance of formality and informality or a somewhat informal service, with 48 percent indicating that 11:00 A.M.worship needed to provide a mix with still more informality.

Responses by length of membership and age were especially revealing. Among those who had been members for five years or less, 79 percent preferred a mix of musical styles in worship, and 73 percent preferred a service that was either a balance of formality and informality or that tended toward informality. Among those who had been members for over five years, however, 64 percent preferred a service with little or no mix of musical styles (28.5 percent wanted no mix at all), and 63.5 percent wanted a service that was either totally or somewhat formal.

Among those under age forty, 78 percent preferred a service with a mix of musical styles, whereas among those forty and older, 56 percent preferred little or no musical mix; 77 percent of respondents under forty liked a service that either balanced formality and informality or tended toward informality, whereas for those forty and over the corresponding figure was 53.5 percent.

All in all, the results confirmed the direction in which we were heading with our 11:00 A.M. service—a mix of musical cultures and a blend of formality and informality. There were clear majorities in favor of even more variety than we were presently offering, and these were especially strong preferences among our younger and newer members.

Still, the question remained, what about the 11 percent who wanted nothing but a totally formal service and the 24.5 percent who wanted no mixture of musical styles whatsoever? Could they recognize that there were others with different needs and preferences from their own, that those others, in fact, constituted a solid majority of the congregation? Could there be for them any compromise, any give-and-take? (Weren't we supposed to learn that in kindergarten?) Could there be any recognition that in the body of Christ we have different members with different preferences and needs, that sharing and affirming our diversity can enrich us all, that none of us should expect to have everything all our own way all the time?

Responses on the preferred method for serving and receiving Holy Communion were illustrative of the challenge. "Always in the pews" was preferred by 22 percent; "usually in the pews" by 19 percent; "a balance" by 35 percent; "usually coming forward" by 20 percent; and "always coming forward" by 4 percent. Obviously, no one approach would satisfy the preferences of a majority. Obviously, many would have to compromise. Such is the challenge of offering people choices, of asking them what they like and what they want. This certainly illustrates why it is so much easier, so much less problematic just to keep on doing things the same old way that you've always done them, even when you're satisfying smaller and smaller numbers of people and your congregation is becoming older and older in the process.

12

The Gathering Storm

Feminists and Pagans

At the outset, 1994 looked like a promising year. We were continuing to enjoy truly significant success in turning around the church's forty years of membership decline, and this would be the year that our strategic plan would be completed. This was also East Liberty's 175th anniversary year and we had planned festive events and projects that had most of us looking forward with eager anticipation.

True, the proposal to merge our trustees and session into one board had been defeated at a special congregational meeting in June of 1993, but that was only by three votes short of the two-thirds majority required. It was also strangely true that the more success we enjoyed, the more persistent and strident were the dissenters' complaints that we were moving in the wrong direction. Once again, however, in my mind, the completion of our strategic plan in mid-1994 held the promise of giving official definition to our mission and vision, carrying the full weight behind it of active congregational participation in the process and session endorsement.

In retrospect, one particular event in early 1994 stands out as a possible harbinger of things to come. It was just after *The Presbyterian Layman,* an unofficial and very conservative publication distributed free of charge throughout our denomination, had published its inflammatory report on "Re-imagining," a theologically controversial ecumenical women's conference that was held in the Twin Cities in November of 1993. At our next session meeting following the appearance of this issue of *The Layman,* a leading member of session (let's call her Marge) made a point of reporting on the Re-imagining event from *The Layman*'s perspective.

This left me somewhat puzzled. As far as I was aware, virtually no one in the congregation took *The Layman* seriously. With the exception of one member who had written the editors a letter of commendation for their journalistic efforts, I had never heard another good word about the publication from any of our church members or officers. Certainly no member of our session had ever quoted or referred to *The Layman* as an authoritative source for anything. As for Marge, a longtime church leader, she and I had worked together compatibly as she served in a variety of capacities right from the start of my ministry at East Liberty. She seemed moderately conservative, but I just couldn't believe that she might be taking her agenda from the pages of *The Layman*.

Fortunately that evening another member of session, a seminary professor, spoke up with a reminder that *The Layman* was a particularly unreliable source with a consistently virulent antifeminist bias. That seemed to lay the matter to rest. No one else had any questions or comments on the subject. We would hear nothing more about Re-imagining at East Liberty until the fall of 1994, when the issue would be raised again in a particularly troublesome way.

In April we enjoyed our big 175th anniversary banquet and celebrated the installation of two beautiful historical displays and exhibit areas in the church. It was also around this time that, still basically trusting her good intent, I asked Marge if she would continue serving in a major leadership role on the session. She agreed. As I recall, it was shortly thereafter that she came to me expressing some concern about the circle dancing that was featured once a month or so at our 9:00 A.M. Sunday Morning Glory Service. The dancing was led each time by a fellow who was part of the Universal Dances of World Peace, a movement that draws on the song and dance traditions of various major world religions. He was also offering the same circle dancing opportunities every Friday evening at the neighboring Friends Meeting House.

I asked Marge what it was that troubled her about these dances. Well, she wasn't quite sure, but there did seem to be something vaguely pagan about it, like something the Druids would do. I pointed out that there are multiple references in the Old Testament to praising God with dance and that folk dancing is to this day still a part of the Jewish religious and cultural tradition. Our conversation didn't go much beyond that. Whether my answer came anywhere near satisfying her, I couldn't say.

Out of the Closet

It was in early 1994 that our search for a new music director became the focus of controversy in a way that none of us had anticipated. It had nothing to do with opposing philosophies of musical tastes or styles. It had to do with sexual orientation. Our search committee had identified a promising candidate who was openly gay. Furthermore, because of his sexual orientation, he had recently been forced out of his position as church organist at a prominent conservative Presbyterian church in another city, where the incident had received major attention in the local news media.

Our candidate flew into Pittsburgh for an initial visit and interview that went very well. All agreed that professionally this was indeed an outstanding candidate. Afterward, a solid majority on the search committee decided that they would like to invite him back for a second visit. Two of the twelve members of the committee were opposed to this candidate, however, on account of his sexual orientation. The search committee decided they should seek the counsel of session. The majority of the committee was, I believe, just as firmly convinced as the two in opposition that this was a matter of conscience, the right thing to do. One of the search committee opponents said she would leave the church if this candidate were invited back.

A special meeting of the session was convened and, with members of the search committee also present and joining in the discussion, the pros and cons of the matter were fully explored. It quickly became clear that I, as staff resource person for the search committee, was to be the opposition's target, even though in reality the committee's enthusiasm for this particular candidate was in no way anything that I had either fostered or engineered. It was simply that most of them were genuinely persuaded of his superior qualifications for the job and were convinced that it would be wrong to disqualify him on account of his sexual orientation.

No matter the truth, one of the opposing search committee members reported to the special session meeting that evening that I had openly admitted that I had a plan to make East Liberty a More Light church (that is, part of a network of Presbyterian congregations that openly declare their intention, in spite of denominational policies to the contrary, to ordain as elders or deacons all qualified candidates without regard to their sexual orientation). I was astounded. The truth was, I promptly responded, that at a recent search committee meeting this same individual who was now falsely accusing me had directly asked me if I had such a plan. Without equivocation I stated that I did not. Shortly thereafter, this same person would proudly confess to me that she was a fundamentalist, the only person in our congregation, to my knowledge, to come out of the theological closet and make that admission. Knowing that she and Marge were close personal friends, I also now had a better fix on where Marge was coming from.

When the vote was taken, by secret ballot, it was 12 to 4 in favor of giving the music director search committee a green light to invite our controversial candidate back for a second interview. Marge wanted the votes of the staff— pastor and associate pastor—reported. However, when the associate pastor immediately objected that this was out of order since the vote had been taken by secret ballot, Marge backed down. I said to myself at the end of that meeting, "Everything from here on will depend on how those four who cast negative votes and the two dissenters on the search committee now handle themselves." I was right about that!

Not long thereafter, a small group of discontented folks gathered to form an East Liberty Church group that took the same name as that of a conservative nationwide organization: Presbyterians for Renewal. The nationwide organization promotes an agenda for the denomination that includes vehement opposition to the ordination of gays and lesbians. Our church group's organizational efforts were bold and aggressive: notices again and again in church publications, placards displayed around the church building. To the group's credit, however, they promptly cautioned those who came to their meetings not to try to make it a forum for open attacks on the pastor because that was not their purpose. Also, in just a few months they decided to drop their original Presbyterians for Renewal tag, having determined, I think, that this gave them too much the appearance of being an organized political opposition. But they did continue to hold regular meetings and to recruit members from the congregation, mostly those of a conservative theological bent.

The Fur Starts to Fly

The session meetings that followed that special meeting, including those at which the final strategic planning committee report was presented, discussed, and acted on, were increasingly difficult and unpleasant. One elder, a longtime, paid member of the choir, falsely accused me of having preached "a series of five or six sermons on homosexuality." The truth was that I had preached only one such sermon. I replied that he was welcome to search my sermon files for those additional sermons and that if he could produce them, I would eat them! Ignoring the offer, he went on to refer to "our next music director, whoever that may be: he, she, or *it*." That was, of course, such an outrageously offensive remark that I should have immediately ruled him out of order. I was, however, simply too shocked to respond at the moment. That same elder then went on to demand disclosure of the amount spent by the search committee to interview the gay candidate, a demand that was properly ignored by the co-chairperson of the search committee who sat on session.

As for the session's consideration of the strategic plan, somewhat surprisingly it was the staffing proposal that became the focus of controversy. The plan called for making permanent the positions of our three part-time pastoral associates, who had for two years been identified as "interim." I was, for several reasons, strongly in support of this proposal. First of all, these three persons were uniquely qualified for the work they were doing. Second, and just as important, they were accomplishing many good things in program areas that were identified as priorities in our strategic plan (as I have previously indicated in chapter 7). Finally, I knew that it was important to the morale of at least two of the three to be finally acknowledged as permanent (even though still part-time) members of our professional ministry and program staff.

The challenge to the staffing plan came from a white male member of session who objected that what the plan was giving us was "three white women." Where was our commitment to racial diversity on our staff? "Perhaps," he stated, "I have too naively trusted staff leadership on this issue." I could see that opposition members on the session were visibly encouraged. Here was an elder who had been a consistent supporter of the senior pastor now seeming to turn against him. I replied to this implied accusation of weak leadership on the issue of staff diversity with a reminder that I had been the one pushing hardest to get our first black associate pastor on the church staff back in 1990. This whole matter was awkward for me, of course, because my wife was one of the three whose positions were under consideration. It would have been even more awkward for me to go on to point out another salient fact about my advocacy for racial diversity on our staff. That was the fact that when the director of our new Family Resource Center and of community mission—a white, male United Methodist minister—had been chosen two years previously, I had been the lone holdout in that search process. Unsuccessfully, I had insisted that we really should have an African American on our staff and in that position.

The strategic plan, *except for the staffing plan*, was approved by the session at its May 1994 meeting. Somehow it seemed like a hollow victory. I was demoralized. My wife was demoralized. Our interim pastoral associate for Taizé and the creative arts was demoralized. An ad hoc committee was pulled together, however, to review the staffing matter and report to session. They recommended acceptance of the proposed staffing plan, pointing out that the plan did clearly state: "As positions on our professional staff may become open in the future, our commitment to diversity within our congregation and lay leadership should apply to the composition of our professional staff as well." At their June meeting the session approved the staffing plan, except that the pastoral associate for Taizé and the creative arts was to remain an interim position until our new music director had arrived and could participate in decisions concerning music and arts department staffing.

Our strategic plan was now officially in place. But morale, trust, and goodwill had been badly shaken by these several conflicted decisions and by the hurtful and false statements made in the process.

From Bad to Worse

Surely God has a sense of humor. The ironies of divine providence can be both bitter and sweet. Our gay candidate for music director withdrew his name from consideration, probably wisely so under the circumstances. In some respects that was a loss for those who opposed him since, unknown to them, his theological background was conservative, evangelical. Theologically he would probably have been more to the liking of his opponents than the man who was ultimately chosen for the position.

Fortunately, we had another top candidate under active consideration whose qualifications were equally outstanding, perhaps superior in certain respects. He was an ordained Presbyterian minister whose overall theological views were probably more compatible with our ministry and program staff and with the dominant culture of the congregation. He was also a highly capable church musician, a product of the Eastman School of Music with many years of experience in urban churches with multicultural congregations. He took to our setting and to our vision for music and the arts like a fish to water. He was also a married man. The subject of sexual orientation never came up in our discussions with him. What we later learned, after he was chosen and had been at work with us for some months, was that he was one of the pioneers of the More Light movement in our denomination! In the 1970s, he was pastor of a church in New Jersey that became just the second in the history of the movement to declare itself a More Light church.

Sadly, by October, when our new music director began his work with us, the conflicts within the congregation had only grown worse. My wife, Jan, found herself challenged by a member of the Christian education committee (we'll call her Leslie) who was also a co-organizer of the initial Presbyterians for Renewal group. Leslie was apparently questioning Jan's integrity by suggesting that Jan, as director of adult education, had intentionally misled the committee by not revealing to them the title of a book that was to be used in a course on feminist theology scheduled for the fall. The course was to be an offering of the Seekers Class, led by a professor of theology at Pittsburgh Theological Seminary who was also a parish associate at East Liberty Church. The book, *She Who Is: The Mystery of God in Feminist Theological Discourse* by Elizabeth A. Johnson, had been, according to Leslie, used at the Re-imagining Conference the previous year.[1]

The facts were that (1) Jan herself did not know what book was to be used, having left that up to the professor who would be teaching the course; (2) the book in question was not used at the Re-imagining Conference; (3) Elizabeth Johnson, a Roman Catholic theologian at Fordham University, is widely regarded as one of the more careful and moderate of feminist theologians; and (4) it was not customary for the Christian education committee to oversee, approve, or disapprove any of the course offerings, topics, or study materials of any of our established adult classes.

The targeting of Jan and *She Who Is* felt like an effort to produce a chilling effect on freedom of intellectual inquiry and discourse in our congregation. But we were not deterred by it. The class went forward with lively discussion and high attendance. At about this same time, however, another charge was leveled. A sister of one of the organizers of our short-lived Presbyterians for Renewal group accused me of reporting false, inflated statistics for summer worship attendance. It was beginning to appear that we had a self-appointed "truth squad" actively at work among us, using tactics not unlike those employed by *The Presbyterian Layman*. It was also around this same time that a small group of old turf men in the congregation began forming a Promise Keepers group.

Right after our new music director arrived in the fall, he made clear his enthusiastic support for retaining the staff position for Taizé and creative arts and making the United Church of Christ minister who had pioneered those ministries a permanent staff member. When I took this recommendation to the personnel committee, however, I ran into a stone wall. Marge was on that committee of four, along with three other longtime, status-quo-oriented members.

None of them attended the Taizé service. None of them much understood or appreciated the kind of change and innovation that the Taizé service represented. Furthermore, in my estimation, they were practicing what could be called "management by gossip." Through their connections in the old turf network of the church they reported hearing unfavorable things about our Taizé minister. They were quite sure that if we recommended to the session that she should be made a permanent staff member, there would be considerable opposition to it. (Some months later, when this same recommendation was put forward by the worship, music, and arts committee, session approved it without a single dissenting vote!)

My spirits and those of other staff members were sinking. I reported this in a personal meeting with the clerk of session and the chairperson of the personnel committee. They, in turn, shared it with the session at their October meeting, after the ministry and program staff had been excused. Following that session meeting, no words of support or encouragement were forthcoming from anyone. One sympathetic, newer member of the church and of the session said to me afterward, "There are some very unlikable, disagreeable people in that group—people that I would not want to spend any more time with than I had to, people that you could never please no matter what you did." Another session member, a longtime church member who had been one of my most consistent and active supporters, was obviously discouraged and dismayed by the tenor of the session's discussion that October evening. "It felt," she said, "like we were going backward to the bad old days at East Liberty." In retrospect, I think it was another of those occasions when the negative few spoke out and the positive majority remained silent.

At the November session meeting, the personnel committee chairperson passed on to me a copy of an anonymous letter that he had just received. It was full of scurrilous attacks on me and another member of the ministry and program staff, and it contained information indicating that the writer was privy to confidential information that could have come only from the church's business office or our budget and finance committee. As if all this were not enough, it was also becoming clear by mid-autumn of 1994 that something of a budget-cutting crusade was being mounted by the budget and finance committee. The charge was being led by the two committee co-chairpersons who were well connected in the old turf network. Stock market performance that year had been flat. So, following the spending formula laid out in our strategic plan, our budget committee co-chairpersons were zealously advocating for deep cuts in the 1995 church budget. I did not resist their conclusion that cuts were needed, but tried my best to moderate the impact on church programs and morale.

There were many tense and lengthy budget meetings in November, December, and early January. Each time we met, the budget and finance committee would present a different set of figures and ratchet up the cutback challenge. Many of us on the ministry and program staff felt that a barely hidden agenda was at work in the budget committee, aggravated by antagonistic attitudes toward staff and an intensely adversarial tone and style. The strategic plan was really the target. Our new Family Resource Center, for example, even though supported by a half-million-dollar foundation grant, was faulted for increasing ancillary church costs. Advertising costs, of course, were a target. Increased spending in music and the arts to support the new program goals endorsed in our strategic plan, goals that our new music director had just been employed to implement, would get the ax. There would be no salary increases for any church staff. The annual church retreat would be eliminated. The 1995 budget would be reduced to 10 percent less than the 1994 budget.

Somewhat oddly, since the story was by then almost four years old, it was our budget battles that would later land us on the front page of the *Wall Street Journal*. Headlined "Rev. Chesnut's Dilemma: A Rich Church and Plenty of Critics," the July 7, 1998, article focused on our 1994–95 conflicts over endowment spending. It seemed strange that the reporter had somehow missed major aspects of a story that should have been of real interest to readers of a business journal. She could have explored, but did not, a church's mission and vision statement and "business" plan that called for a rather explicit entrepreneurial strategy. She could have told, but did not, the story of a declining, tradition-bound, organizational behemoth that had been turned around through the successful application of marketing precepts to identify and reach new market segments. In retrospect it was clear that the journalist had come looking for a story of church conflict over money. Unable to see beyond her own parameters, that was the story she found and that was the story she told. Disappointing. But then, how many ministers make it to the front page of the *Wall Street Journal* . . . unless they're going to jail!

My morale was at rock bottom. My resiliency was depleted. The completion and approval of our strategic plan had not brought us together as I had hoped. Out of all the discouraging developments, probably the most demoralizing of all was the fact that a handful of our relatively newer and younger members were actively involved in the opposition leadership. They had, of course, gotten their orientation to church life through their connections in the old turf network. All along I had been counting on the support of our increasing number of new members to move forward our innovative vision as developed in the strategic plan.

As 1994 drew to a close, my spirits badly sagging, I was beginning to conclude that I had done all I could at East Liberty Church. For my own well-being, it seemed that I had better start considering the possibility of a call to another church.

13

Annus Horribilis

From Cathedral of Hope
to Temple of Doom?

Queen Elizabeth II of England declared 1992 the royal family's *annus horribilis*, their "horrible year." It was in that year that each of the queen's three married children either separated or divorced and the royal residence at Windsor Castle was devastated by fire. For East Liberty Presbyterian Church our horrible year was 1995. The second half of 1994 had been bad enough, but 1995 was definitely our *annus horribilis*.

Toward the end of 1994 I shared with a handful of individuals that I was, sadly and reluctantly, starting to look around for another pastorate. By the time we held our church officers retreat in the spring of 1995, word of this had begun to circulate to a few others. The retreat was a horrible experience for me. Feelings were still raw and relationships tense from our recent budget battles. On Friday evening when we broke into small groups, I found myself, by the luck of the draw, included in a group that was dominated by three of my fiercest critics. None, by the way, was a longtime church member; two had joined the church since I had become pastor. These three promptly turned the discussion into an inquisition. Why was I doing this, why was I doing that? Why Matthew Fox, feminist theology, the New Age sermon series? Other members of the group sat in stunned silence. It was not said in so many words, but the underlying tenor of the questions seemed to suggest some doubt as to whether or not I was truly a Christian. Later I would hear that there were those in the opposition who were making this very accusation, "Chesnut is *not* a Christian."

On Saturday, one of the retreat participants openly raised the question as to whether or not it was true that the senior pastor was considering leaving, and, if so, why? As I recall, I responded something to the effect that I didn't think that this was the time or the place to answer that. The fat, however, was now in the fire. Special session meetings were called soon thereafter to explore what was going on. A conflict resolution consultant was called in on short notice for one special meeting, but to little avail. Accusations were flying back and forth. Battle lines were hardening, opposing camps forming, and confusion spreading within the congregation among the vast majority who had little or no idea until now that anything was at all wrong. After a year of prolonged agony that had been a double dose for my wife and me since she was also serving on the church staff, Jan made her own sad and reluctant decision to resign her part-time position in May.

I decided to ask the session for a four-month sabbatical, from July through October, in order to get some time for rest, renewal, and reflection. I was now into my seventh year at ELPC, and the need for respite seemed timely, to say the least. The session approved and sent out a letter to the congregation (drafted by Marge and full of affirmation of my ministry!) that explained a bit about my request for a sabbatical and invited members of the congregation to an open meeting where I would tell them more and respond to their questions. At that meeting I was, to put it mildly, faced with the challenge of performing a high-wire act, trying to say just enough to make some sense of what had been going on behind the scenes at the church without further inflaming our multiple and complex points of conflicts.

Now why on earth, you may wonder, would Marge write a letter to the congregation lauding my ministry? In retrospect, I believe that she and other members of her camp believed that they had won their war of attrition, that I would be soon gone. Being in the minority, however, they did not want it to appear that they had been responsible for bringing about my departure. For one thing, a number of them had been on the pastor search committee that had brought me to East Liberty. So the story line they were now advancing was that I had done an admirable job during my ministry at the church, accomplishing many good things at a time when my kind of ministry was what the doctor ordered. But that era in the church's history, according to their story line, had now come and gone. It was time for Chesnut and for the church to move on, each in new and different directions. And it was time—they could have added, if they had been fully honest about it—for them "to get *their* church back."

Marge and her cohorts had another good reason not to appear responsible for the end of my pastorate at East Liberty. A new group of supporters for the vision articulated in our strategic plan and for my leadership was emerging, mainly from the Seekers Class. These folks were beginning to write letters of concern to session and to show up as observers at session meetings. This was nothing that I had organized or instigated, but their calm and steady, constructive and persistent show of support was most welcome. Some of the leaders of this support group were professionals in various fields of organizational behavior. They possessed a clear and steady vision of what they were doing and they did it in an effective, noninflammatory way. These were not individuals acting out their own personal psychodramas in public conflict. They were simply people standing up and speaking out for a vision they shared, for a style of ministry and a way of "being church" in which they believed. I firmly believe that without the emergence of this group of active and effective supporters our story would have had a very different outcome.

The struggle, however, was just beginning. Once I was on sabbatical, the opponents on session became increasingly bold, perhaps partly because they saw that now that I had a group of effective and organized supporters, my departure might not be such a sure thing after all. Maybe I would be encouraged to stay on. Maybe it would be necessary after all to push me out. So session conflicts grew increasingly intense through the summer months. A tug-of-war saw first one side prevail, then the other. At no time did the opposition count more than one-third of the session solidly on its side. But once again, because it was the opposition that was most outspoken and had worked up the strongest negative head of steam, because their leaders on session were coming to meetings with an agenda prepared beforehand, and because those of the moderate middle were much more passive and reluctant to engage in struggle, a seesaw dynamic was evident in session votes.

One of the budget committee co-chairpersons who sat on session drafted a resolution that would have recommended to the congregation that my pastoral relationship with the congregation be, as Presbyterians put it, "dissolved" at the end of my sabbatical. That was quickly squelched, but another motion put forward by the same individual did prevail for a short while, a resolution that barred me from the church building during my sabbatical and forbade me to have any contact with the individuals who were supporting me! If they couldn't banish me, at least they would exile me for a time! (What next, I wondered, house arrest?) This move too, however, was short-lived. Gentle persuasion by the Seekers support group convinced a majority of the session that this move was unwise and unwarranted. At the next meeting session reversed itself on this "exile" resolution.

Getting Outside Help

How did I survive this ordeal, this apparent death of a dream to which I had devoted myself heart, mind, and soul for seven long years? The comfort and support of family and friends was key. Taizé prayers helped. Reading the laments, complaints, and prayers of the psalms helped. Never before had I appreciated, as I now did, what had previously struck me as the paranoia of many psalms, their seeming obsession with deliverance from enemies and foes:

> The LORD is my light and my salvation;
>   whom shall I fear?
> The LORD is the stronghold of my life;
>   of whom shall I be afraid?
> When evildoers assail me
>   to devour my flesh—

my adversaries and foes—
    they shall stumble and fall.
Though an army encamp against me,
    my heart shall not fear;
though war rise up against me,
    yet I will be confident. . . .
Now my head is lifted up
    above my enemies all around me. . . .
Do not give me up to the will of my adversaries,
    for false witnesses have risen against me,
    and they are breathing out violence. . . .
Wait for the LORD;
    be strong, and let your heart take courage;
    wait for the LORD!
                    (Psalm 27:1–3, 6a, 12, 14)

It also helped my morale immensely that I was receiving many expressions of interest from search committees coast to coast. From March through November of 1995, I had the opportunity to consider seriously over two dozen congregations searching for a senior pastor. With ten of them I had on-site visits. Their interest, of course, was encouraging. The process of reading their search materials and visiting with their search committees was both an instructive exercise and a morale-boosting diversion from the agonies back home in Pittsburgh.

What was not so encouraging, however, either about these new "opportunities" or about the state of the church at large, was discovering how many of these rather prominent congregations had recently suffered or were presently suffering their own internal conflicts and divisions. Some situations were as bad as, if not worse than, those at East Liberty. Two congregations had recently lost their pastors due to sexual misconduct. One appeared to be a "serial clergy killer" congregation. At another, the founding pastor, who had retired five years previously, was still on the scene, trying to influence church affairs, even though this had caused his successor to depart after just three years. In addition, even among the healthy congregations, not a single one of these churches gave any evidence that they had undertaken or had much interest in undertaking anything particularly innovative—nothing like the new, groundbreaking ministries that we were developing at East Liberty. Finally, in many instances I sensed that their search committees were intentionally made up of representatives of the various factions in their congregations. What they were looking for, therefore, was someone who would please everyone, someone who would not rock their already rocky boats.

The East Liberty session was also looking outside for help. They decided to call in a consultant in church conflict resolution. Marge was to make the arrangements and I was to be involved in choosing the consultant. But that was not quite how it was done. The consultant was chosen—Hugh Halverstadt of

McCormick Theological Seminary in Chicago—and the times were set for his visits to the church without my ever being involved. Marge informed me of it all after the arrangements were finalized. Unfortunately, Halverstadt would be coming to East Liberty Church to interview people over two successive weekends at the very time that Jan and I had made plans for a two-week trip south. Our schedule was to include participating in a spiritual life workshop at our national Presbyterian conference center in Montreat, North Carolina. We were registered for a very timely workshop entitled "When the Bottom Drops Out!" Given Hugh's tight schedule, the only way Jan and I could make our input into the process was to fly to Chicago to meet with him in his office there, prior to our trip to North Carolina. In Chicago, I told Hugh I thought the situation at East Liberty looked pretty bleak. As for my being able to return to my ministry there, I said, it looked pretty much like trying to put Humpty-Dumpty back together again.

Our time at Montreat was very well spent. It gave Jan and me opportunity to share our troubles in a supportive group of others going through their own hard times. It gave me a spiritually healing time and space to write some of my own psalms of lament, complaint, and cries for deliverance. Meanwhile, back at East Liberty, Halverstadt, after having interviewed about forty individuals of various viewpoints, was making his report to the session. The congregation was invited to listen in and eventually to join in the discussion. Fortunately, Hugh did not try to make much use of his own complex theories developed in his book *Managing Church Conflict.*[1] Instead, he simply applied his skills of astute personal observation and organizational analysis plus a good measure of basic common sense. No blame was placed on any person, party, or faction. There was no big focus on the pastor, simply an indication that it would be best for all concerned if the pastor's future with the congregation were to be resolved one way or another as soon as possible. It was now early September. I knew that soon I had to come to a decision whether to resign without having a new call in hand or to return to my beleaguered pastorate at East Liberty. The former felt like leaping off a cliff, the latter like jumping back into the inferno.

In October, with less than a month left in my sabbatical, the session invited me to meet with a small group of elders of my choosing who, together with representatives of the presbytery's Committee on Ministry, would discuss with me my responses to Hugh Halverstadt's report and recommendations. It was an anguishing decision, but still convinced of the Humpty-Dumpty factor, I went to that meeting with my letter of resignation in hand, presenting it at the outset. Nearly all present seemed to be approaching the subject with an open mind, inclined to think it through at length and explore other options as well.

It was our seminary professor on session who began to make a persuasive case for my staying on and giving it one more good try, even if just for a few more months. "Look," he argued, "the Halverstadt report has given us some very objective goals on which to focus. The pastor can lead session through the process laid out in those recommendations and we can begin to turn this situation around. I say there is no need for the pastor to resign. If he does, following this kind of trouble, it will probably be several years before we find another pastor, and who's to guarantee that we will find one who's as good a fit for this congregation as the one we now have? Much of what we've worked so hard to achieve here could all be undone." The tide of opinion began to turn in this direction. I too was eventually persuaded that this was the way to go. We surely could not expect it would be easy and there would be no guarantees that it would work. Christians, however, of all people, ought to believe in the possibilities of resurrection and reconciliation.

It Wasn't Easy

During the late summer and early fall of 1995, while I was still on sabbatical, another point of discord was erupting at East Liberty Church. Once again, it was music and involved the choir. Even with his pastoral, caring spirit and his steady, patient efforts to bring the recalcitrant ones around during his first year with us, our new music director had not succeeded. Most of our paid choir members and many of the volunteers would still not support the new directions for music set forth in our strategic plan. The director was still being met with resistance, hostility, and outright defiance. So, displaying as much courage as he had pastoral care, he bit the bullet. There would be big changes: no paid soloists and no pay for members of the church who sang in the choir. There would continue to be paid positions for section leaders and some other singers, but those with bad attitudes and poor attendance were terminated. The immediate result was that our choir was decimated. Not only were most of the paid singers gone, so were many of the volunteer singers who quit in protest. Yes, it surely had to be done and it was done the best way possible, but it still hurt. Altogether, we probably lost as many people over this episode as for any other single cause.

So, it was back into this seething cauldron that I stepped. Even before that, at a special session meeting called in late October to discuss the smaller group's conclusion that I should return to my post, three or four opposition session members had put me on the rack for another inquisition. For the most part, the rest of the elders sat through it all in passive silence. That experience certainly gave me strong second thoughts about returning, but I would stick to my commitment to give it another solid try. If, however, I had often felt before that I was walking through a minefield in my work, it was doubly so now.

The months to follow, even the next couple of years were not easy. Some of our dissidents had given up, some had gone away, a few were making conscientious efforts to reconcile, but some of the diehards also hung in there, ready to jump back into the fray whenever opportunities presented themselves. One of these was Judd, the fellow who had taken it upon himself to go to presbytery officials to demand the reinstatement of our associate pastor even while he was still under investigation for misconduct. Judd was not and never had been a church officer at East Liberty. His consistent pattern was to go around the process, to whisper his concerns around the edges, to go over the heads and around the backs of church leadership.

Another still active dissident was Clarence, the individual who had been characterized, even by fellow conservatives, as "somewhere to the right of Attila the Hun." This man, who had rotated back and forth for years as a member of trustees and of session, had long been a negative influence in church life. Clarence and Judd are, in fact, the two most compulsively oppositional individuals I have ever known in my life. Clarence had finally shown his true colors in public at the congregational forum that was called to hear and discuss Hugh Halverstadt's report. His strident and intemperate comments on that occasion had actually done himself and the opposition's cause far more harm than good. Some of those who had not known much about what was going on could now witness for themselves the nature of the opposition with which we had long been struggling behind the scenes. Nevertheless, over a year following my return to ministry at East Liberty, Clarence wrote a lengthy letter to session attacking the directions of my leadership. It was also, true to form, strident, intemperate, and inaccurate, again doing Clarence and his cause far more harm than good. This time the session unanimously responded with reproof and admonition to the writer to be more careful, both about his tone and about the truth.

Clarence and Marge (who still had a year and a half to serve on the session following my return), however, and others of the old turf network were also now setting their sights on our new music director. His session-approved campaign to raise funds for a grand piano to provide appropriate support for greater musical variety in our sanctuary service was being attacked and undermined first at one point then at another. In the midst of it all, a lightning strike put our organ out of commission one weekend, making it abundantly clear that it would be useful to have a grand piano as a backup instrument. Marge then went so far as to accuse the music director (to his face but not in public) of having sabotaged the organ in order to further his plans to get a piano! Simultaneously, Clarence and a relative (ordinarily, these two were not on such good terms with one another), both of whom had long sung in the choir, were trumping up distorted charges with the trustees' property committee that the music director was neglecting proper care of the organ and other church musical instruments. The open conflict by now was pretty much past, but it looked like we were back into that low-intensity war of attrition. How long, O Lord?

14

Putting Humpty-Dumpty Together Again

Consulting and Discerning

Sometimes I feel that I have acquired enough experience with consultants to become a consultant on consultants. As a result of recommendations by our conflict resolution consultant Hugh Halverstadt, additional consultants were called in during 1996 and 1997 in the areas of church communications, personnel, and staff team building. Plus, on our own initiative, we invited a consultant from our denominational staff in Louisville to lead a workshop on peacemaking in the local church. None of these consultants did us any harm and most of them were at least modestly helpful, though in my opinion none of them told us much that we—at least those close to the heart of church affairs— did not already know. On the other hand, it was admittedly useful to have experienced, knowledgeable, and objective outsiders confirming the importance of certain points on which there was not general agreement within the church or among our leadership. For example, both the communications and the personnel consultants urged us to revisit the structural issue of merging our session and trustees into one board.

In my estimation, one of the most helpful developments of all grew from a seed planted by my wife a couple of years previously. Having met the Rev. Chuck Olsen during a denominational conference for spiritual directors held at our national Presbyterian conference center in Montreat, North Carolina, Jan had made me aware of Chuck's pioneering work out of his Center for Worshipful Work in Kansas City. The author of *Transforming Church Boards into Communities of Spiritual Leaders*, Chuck is making a transforming contribution to America's mainline churches by teaching us to approach the way we conduct our church decision making as a uniquely spiritual process that does not just mimic the business procedures of corporate America.[1]

We invited Chuck to East Liberty Presbyterian Church in the spring of 1996 and again in the spring of 1997, both times to lead a retreat for our church officers—elders, deacons, and trustees—and program staff. As a result of Chuck's guidance and vision our session meetings became more spiritual and worshipful experiences with frequent opportunities for prayer and song and ritual and personal sharing structured into our agendas.

Our communications consultant gave us a meeting evaluation questionnaire that we used regularly at our session meetings. At each meeting we discussed the results, assessing whether or not we were making progress on our process goals, and we sought to encourage more equality of participation in our meetings by giving each elder a fixed number of tokens at the outset of the meeting. Each time an individual made a contribution, he or she was to surrender a token until his or her supply was depleted. That elder was then to remain silent until others had an opportunity to be heard. All of this was noticeably beneficial in bringing a better spirit and more constructive attitudes to our meetings.

Chuck Olsen's center trains church leaders as "discernmentarians." Chuck believes, and I agree, that parliamentary debate and procedure are often divisive and counterproductive methods of making decisions and resolving church disputes. The discernment process aims to discern the will of God rather than simply to determine the will of the majority. It seeks to discover and to build a spiritually derived consensus that, even if it does not arrive at 100 percent agreement, will at least permit a solid majority to move ahead without resentment or resistance from the minority even when the minority cannot wholeheartedly support the majority's conclusions.

In 1997 we put the discernment process to the test on the issue of whether or not we should merge our session and trustees into one board. Church officers and members were invited to participate in an all-day Saturday session on "Discerning the United Board Question." Leadership was provided by yet another consultant, a Methodist minister from neighboring Ohio. An Olsen-trained discernmentarian, she did a superb job. By the end of the day we were still not all in agreement on the substance of the issue. However, we were able to support a recommendation to the session that the matter should once again be put to a vote of the congregation at the next annual meeting. A second recommendation was made that there should be plenty of opportunity for open discussion of the issues in congregational forums held in advance of the annual meeting.

An Inclusive Church Is Not for Everyone

Other steps also proved constructive in bringing our congregation back together around a renewed sense of shared identity. During 1996 and into 1997, I offered a series of approximately sixteen sermons organized around the overall theme, "Rediscovering Our Mainline Christian Identity," with four subheadings: Our Hebrew Roots; Our Christian Origins; Our Catholic Tradition; and Our Reformation Heritage. It was an effort to sketch the big picture of Christian faith from the perspective of a contemporary, ecumenical, progressive Protestantism that is firmly planted in but not slavishly bound by scripture and tradition.

Simultaneously, we offered an adult education series on our Presbyterian approach to theological unity and diversity. It was led by one of our congregation's theologians from nearby Pittsburgh Seminary and utilized an officially approved denominational study document entitled *Is Christ Divided?* I think it was helpful for some of our conservative dissidents to read there: "When love leads to a community of theological discourse, there is no prior restriction of theological proposals. *Even views which strike some as outrageous are no longer occasion for hasty condemnation* but rather for careful theological exploration which seeks to build the church in faithfulness." The peace we seek in the church, the report declares, "is not the pretense of theological agreement or the avoidance of theological conflict. It is *the open acknowledgment of differences which can be addressed in love* so that the community may be built up in faith, hope, and love."[2]

Beginning in the fall of 1997 and continuing into 1999, we sponsored a guest preacher series featuring the presidents of our Presbyterian Church (U.S.A.) theological seminaries who were asked to address the topic "Theological Unity and Diversity in the Presbyterian Church Today: What Is Our Common Ground?" As we moved into 1999, we began offering our guest preachers the option of speaking either on this topic or on "Our Presbyterian Approach to Biblical Interpretation and Authority." This latter topic is one on which we have not one but two officially approved denominational study documents,[3] so in January of 1999 these documents were used as the basis of a very well-attended adult series taught by another of our Pittsburgh Seminary theologians in the congregation.

There are certain inevitable, built-in contradictions, of course, in the quest for unity in diversity. Alexander Campbell, one of the nineteenth-century founders of the Christian Church (Disciples of Christ) movement for American Christian unity, advanced the admirable motto: "In essentials unity, in nonessentials liberty, in all things charity." Campbell and many of his compatriots were former Scots Presbyterians who were fed up with the bitter, petty doctrinal disputes and schisms that were especially characteristic of the Western Pennsylvania Presbyterianism of their time—disputes, for example, over whether musical instruments were acceptable in Christian worship. Campbellites sought to rally Christians of all denominations around a few essentials of New Testament belief and practice.

The trick, of course, is to agree about what are the essentials versus the nonessentials of faith and practice. Disputing over what matters and what does not, you often find that charity and unity are lost once more. One of the wings of Campbell's new movement for Christian unity, for example, soon split off from the rest—and from all other Christians as well—on the basis of their insistence that no true church of Christ could allow the use of instrumental music in

Christian worship. And there you are again, right back into petty disputes and schisms with plenty of variety but precious little unity or charity.

Our congregation's one openly professed fundamentalist charged me with being tolerant of everyone except fundamentalists. Is that like being accused of being intolerant of intolerance? If so, then I suppose I must confess to it. If you have a congregation whose leadership is committed to drawing the circle of love large enough to include all who seek to be included—specifically, let's say, people of various sexual orientations, or those who like a variety of musical styles—do you not inevitably exclude those who would insist on drawing the circle much smaller? Well, not necessarily. A tolerant majority may respect a less tolerant minority *provided that* the minority also respects the majority and does not insist on holding a veto over majority decisions.

Obviously, however, in a congregation that values diversity and inclusivity, a minority of 10 percent to 15 percent who insist that nothing else is acceptable but high-church, sacred classical music cannot be allowed to have it their way exclusively. Most likely, those who want to draw the circle much smaller and tighter will eventually exclude themselves from the large-circle congregation. They will find another congregation where their views prevail. That's why I say realistically, but admittedly somewhat sadly, "An inclusive church is not for everyone."

Sociologist Nancy Ammerman notes in her study of congregations in changing communities that many of those congregations that face up squarely to their own need to change with their changing environments will inevitably go through painful splits. That did not happen at East Liberty. This could have been partly due to the fact that our dissenters never did amount to more than 15 percent or so of the congregation, though they were somewhat overrepresented in leadership positions where they might have held closer to 30 percent of the spots on the session and 50 percent or so on the board of trustees.

Not surprisingly, some of our dissenters did withdraw, trickling off to other congregations where they were more comfortable, perhaps thirty or forty of them during 1996–97. About an equal number have remained affiliated with our congregation to one degree or another. Many of these have retreated to their various familiar corners in what remains of the church's old turf network, attending one or another of our weekly services if and when the senior pastor is not preaching there. Some will speak when spoken to. Some, I suspect, are waiting it out until I die or retire, at which time they probably expect to get their church back. I still get reports from time to time of vicious things said about me behind my back or, along with our music director, may receive an anonymous communication signed "The ELPC Underground." Most disturbing of all— after one recent tussle with a certain member who had admitted to me that she loved a good fight, there appeared, taped on our front door one night, an anonymous note that read in bold, crayon print: You Unimaginable Bastard. My wife and I were out of town at the time. Our adult daughter, who was home alone in our large house, was scared half to death when she left for work in the morning and found this hateful message stuck to our door. She called us long distance, wondering if she should report this frightening, abusive incident to the police.

During our times of toughest trouble and afterward, I did keep trying to reach out to many—but admittedly not all—of those on the other side who seemed like they might be open to reconciling initiatives. My wife and I had some of them to dinner where we invited open discussion of our disagreements. Others I treated to lunch or visited in their home. Some I simply called to see how they were doing or to offer them some opportunity or another to participate in church life. Many of these efforts were fruitless. Quite a few were rebuffed. Very few such initiatives were made in our direction.

There has been at least one notable exception. Much to her credit, Leslie, one of the women who was involved in organizing the Presbyterians for Renewal group, did later make repeated and conscientious efforts toward dialogue and reconciliation. She even apologized once. She has stayed involved and made numerous positive contributions. Commendably, she has kept on stretching and growing in her own views, though she also still feels free to say so when she disagrees. Sadly, she's been one of a rare breed among our dissenters.

Moving On with Bold New Decisions

Eventually our strategic plan did provide the focal point for unity that I had long hoped for. We have kept it before our congregation. We have made single-sheet versions of our mission and vision statement, core values, priorities, and goals available to visitors and new members. We have posted enlarged copies of the same material around the church building "that those who run may read." The strategic plan has been reviewed and discussed in annual new officer training sessions. We have devoted a whole year in session meetings to month-by-month review of the plan's ongoing implementation. Every week on each of our worship service bulletins we highlight a boxed statement excerpted from our plan that reads: *"Our congregation seeks to promote peace, justice, and human dignity; to reflect a spirit of openness, sharing and learning in our ministry and mission; to build a richly diverse faith community that witnesses to our oneness in Christ across all boundaries of race, social class, culture, gender, and lifestyle."*

We really moved on rather rapidly after the conflicts of 1994–95 to become the congregation that our strategic plan envisions. Once unencumbered of a relatively small number of relentless obstructionists, we were able to take certain steps that previously would have been highly controversial and conflict-filled decisions. Our congregation had finally become free to claim and to fulfill its inherent identity and mission. For example, our new director of music and the arts was soon proposing that we offer the Renaissance City Choirs of Pittsburgh, Pittsburgh's premier gay and lesbian choral groups, a home base as artists in residence at East Liberty Church. The session approved unanimously.

In 1997 the Presbyterian Church (U.S.A.) approved the so-called Amendment B, a measure that was largely aimed at disqualifying self-professing, sexually active homosexual persons from ordination as ministers, elders, or deacons. In response, our justice and global concerns committee proposed a statement to the session that, with minor amendment, was unanimously approved and sent out to our congregation. That statement read in part: "The policy of the church is to welcome all into membership. . . . Our unique, metropolitan membership should not be concerned that East Liberty Presbyterian Church will regress from its policies of inclusiveness in the whole life of the church. Our commitment is to diversity of opinion and membership." This was supported with references to our mission and vision statement in the strategic plan.

The following year our session endorsed the statement of purpose of a newly organized, nationwide group called the Covenant Network of Presbyterians on whose national committee I was serving. The session also committed $10,000 to support the Covenant Network's effort to overturn Amendment B and to work toward a truly inclusive church.

It has helped immensely that from our period of intense conflict to the present we have had a succession of chairpersons of our church nominating committee who have held firm to the convictions that we need: (1) lay leaders who share the church's mission and vision adopted with the strategic plan in 1994; (2) equal representation of both newer and longer-time members; (3) rotation of officers to give those a break who have had more than their share of turns on our boards; and (4) leaders who—whatever their viewpoints—are basically open-minded, constructive, and cooperative rather than compulsively oppositional.

New leadership on our budget and finance committee provided immense relief and improvement in our budget development processes and attitudes. Gone were the intensely adversarial, divisive budget discussions. Budget meetings open to all were now held to hear and discuss committee budget proposals for the coming year. Everyone felt that they could get a fair hearing. Mission and vision priorities in the strategic plan were the guiding factor, not the private agendas of individual budget committee members. Still, fiscal responsibility was honored. From 1995 through 1997, overall church spending remained below the 1994 level, even as the endowment continued to grow in real dollar value.

I have long believed that one of the great unifying forces in our congregation has been the high degree to which our ministry and program staff has shared core beliefs, values, and visions. Yes, some of our relationships were strained during the time of worst conflict, but since that time we have been aided immensely by a capable, caring, proactive personnel committee chaired by an elder with many years of professional personnel experience. As individual staff members we may be very different in our personality types and work styles, we may from time to time bump up against one another and step on each other's toes, yet we agree on which way is north for the church of Jesus Christ. We have been solidly united in our commitment to the church's strategic plan, to its mission and vision. We sometimes experience the joy of creating synergy together. We hold each other in high mutual esteem, respect, and affection. We work together as a collegial team. As leader of the team responsible for oversight, I also try not to be looking over the shoulders of our staff constantly, to get myself out of the way when appropriate, to step in with advice or guidance when needed, to support a climate of trust and empowerment.

Finally, in late 1997, our session and trustees in a joint meeting unanimously voted to recommend to the congregation to merge these two boards into one. Not surprisingly, several church members we had not seen for a long time showed up for the vote at our February 1998 congregational meeting. The proposal, however, was approved by a majority of three-fourths. What a relief! We had finally gotten past that built-in structure for conflict and confusion that had so long plagued our church governance and decision-making processes. Session meetings ever since have been a joy and delight.

In my 1997 annual report to the congregation, I wrote: "I believe we have come through our past times of trouble with a new determination not to be distracted from our mission, with a stronger sense of our identity, and with new energy for moving on to fulfill our calling and our potential. . . . It is very gratifying that we have neither abandoned nor retreated from our vision and that we are now pressing forward with renewed enthusiasm. Our future looks bright with God's promise."

PART III

Transforming the Church
for a New Millennium

For there is still a vision for the appointed time; . . .
If it seems to tarry, wait for it;
 it will surely come, it will not delay.
 —Habakkuk 2:3

Let anyone who has an ear listen to what the Spirit
is saying to the churches. . . . "See, I am making all
things new."
 —Revelation 2:17; 21:5

15

Back to the Vision

The Labyrinth: Reaching Out to Pilgrims

My approach after returning from the four-month sabbatical in late 1995 was to steer our church ship "steady as she goes" and generally along the same course that we had consistently taken since my arrival in 1988. That meant taking no heedless steps to irritate traditionalists, all the while firmly pursuing a course of thoughtful innovation that had become our Cathedral of Hope hallmark. So, for example, when Jan told me in early 1996 that she was interested in sharing with our Seekers Class the recently rediscovered medieval practice of walking cathedral labyrinths as a form of "prayer in motion," I initially expressed some reservation. Would our traditionalists see it as yet one more troubling, New Age, trendy, neo-pagan fad? (Yes, of course, they would.) Jan believed it offered healing potential for the congregation—a newly rediscovered ancient Christian spiritual practice that could help to bring us all back together. Whatever our traditionalists might make of it, however, I was convinced that the labyrinth offered such a powerful metaphor of spiritual journey that it could be an effective instrument for reaching out to some of the very people we were trying to reach.

Within a few months, Jan had organized a task force of Seekers Class volunteers and others who joined together in fabricating a beautiful canvas replica of the original labyrinth pattern as laid into the stone floor nave of Chartres Cathedral in the twelfth century. Like the original, at a full forty feet in diameter, our Cathedral of Hope version was also a marvelous work of both art and geometry. The work itself was directed by one of our newer members, a young man in his early thirties, a professional in the field of sets and costumes at the drama department of Carnegie Mellon University. Volunteer painters, seamstresses, and carpenters (who constructed a wooden platform on which the canvas was laid out for work) all united in a truly communal effort.

We dedicated and inaugurated our Cathedral of Hope Labyrinth at a special Sunday evening chapel service in September 1996. Following the dedication service, the labyrinth was laid out for walking under the stars in the church garth, our beautiful interior courtyard. By torch and candlelight, to the accompaniment of Gregorian chant, more than 150 persons—many of them first-time visitors to East Liberty—walked the labyrinth that lovely Indian summer evening. On six successive Sunday evenings thereafter labyrinth walks were scheduled following a discussion group that focused on the book *Walking a Sacred Path: Rediscovering the Labyrinth as a Spiritual Tool,* by the Rev. Dr. Lauren Artress.[1] Artress, canon of Grace Episcopal Cathedral in San Francisco, is the "mother" of the recent rediscovery of the labyrinth as an ancient Christian aid to prayer and meditation, a symbolic spiritual journey, a pilgrimage to the Holy City. We were delighted, by the way, to have Lauren Artress lead weekend workshops at East Liberty Church in the fall of 1999.

We estimate that close to two thousand individuals walked our Cathedral of Hope Labyrinth in 1998. It has become one of our major means of outreach to spiritually sensitive, seeking individuals and organizations receptive to old, yet new, expressions of spiritual renewal and quest. The pilgrimage metaphor is equally compatible with traditional biblical imagery and with New Age sensitivities. It also fits beautifully with our Cathedral of Hope approach to spirituality as a journey, a lifelong process. The highly personal, individual nature of the experience speaks to both baby boomer and Generation X mind-sets. We gently seek to set the experience within the context of Christian faith and community, yet each individual is ultimately free to make of it what she or he will.

Taizé Blossoms

From year to year since its founding in 1992, our Wednesday evening Taizé service has grown, both in numbers and in its impact on church life. By 1998 the service was attracting an average of 75 to 80 worshipers a week. During that same year, 25 percent of our new members and friends who affiliated with East Liberty Church told us that they had first come into the church through the Taizé service. Because we have many worshipers at this service who are active in their own congregations elsewhere (many are Roman Catholic), we carefully avoid any heavy-handed approach to new member recruitment. At the same time, we run a regular welcome to visitors in the Taizé worship bulletin that states: "You are welcome at any of our programs and worship services. It is possible to have more than one church home. If you are interested in becoming a member or friend of this church, please speak to one of our pastors." Also, every six weeks or so our associate pastor is present to offer a newcomers orientation to ELPC following the Taizé service for those who are interested.

In 1994 we took a significant step with our Taizé service, a step that I believe has been an essential element in the enduring and growing appeal of the service. At each Wednesday evening service we began extending an invitation to those who wished to come forward, while the prayerful singing continued, quietly to share prayer requests and then to receive anointing, the laying on of hands, and prayers for healing and wholeness. At every service at the appointed time a line forms in the center aisle of our chapel. At least a dozen persons and sometimes many more are waiting to receive this healing ministry from a member of our staff or one of our lay leaders.

As one who takes my own turn in offering this healing ministry, I can testify that it has been one of the most spiritually and emotionally moving experiences of my entire thirty-seven years as an ordained minister. Now that we have an active corps of Stephen Ministers (church members who receive special training in lay pastoral care giving) in the congregation, we have begun to offer, following the Taizé service, an opportunity for individual worshipers to meet and share their concerns with a sympathetic, caring listener.

Another popular expression of "embodied spirituality" we have offered is candlelight processions through our darkened cathedral, singing Taizé prayers as we go, marking high points of the Christian year such as Epiphany, Ash Wednesday, Holy Saturday, and All Saints' and/or All Souls' Day. Our "interactive" stations of the cross offered on Good Friday and Holy Saturday are also well attended.

The Soul Center Surprise

Cast your bread upon the water and it shall return unto you. Give and you shall receive. A cathedral ministry is, in large part, about offering your ministry to the benefit of a whole metropolitan region, often without any clear return. That's the way it is with our Taizé and labyrinth ministries that serve many members and clergy of other churches who will never become members of East Liberty Church. Yet the promise of scripture is that when we sow generously we shall reap generously. Give your life away, said Jesus, and you will find it.

Our Taizé and Cathedral of Hope Labyrinth ministries inspired just such a dynamic in one particularly astonishing way. One of our quiet visitors to Taizé services and labyrinth walks was a minister, not affiliated with our church, who was working on a Ph.D. in spiritual formation at Duquesne University in Pittsburgh, an individual who happens also to be independently wealthy. So impressed was she with our Taizé and labyrinth ministries and with the classes and workshops in spirituality we were also offering on Wednesday evenings, that she decided to celebrate the attainment of her doctoral degree in the spring of 1997 in a most unusual way. She proposed to give East Liberty Church a special gift of at least $36,000 annually over the next fifteen years for the establishment of a spiritual life center!

This all seemed doubly providential because just a few months before her generous offer and completely unknown to our benefactor, I had lifted up a dream in my annual report to the congregation:

> Among the many things we Presbyterians have been good at are the
> institutional and organizational and the intellectual-theological aspects

of our faith. In recent years, however, there has been a growing awareness that simply going through the liturgical and intellectual motions
of religion can still leave the spirit dry and barren, untouched by God
and the gospel. There are many, many hungry hearts in search of a faith
community that will assist and guide them in feeding their spirits with
the Spirit of the living God.

In this same piece I went on to report some counsel that I had received in
personal correspondence with Lyle Schaller a few years earlier. Schaller had
indicated to me that in his opinion the most promising future course for our
congregation lay in developing our potential as a regional center for spiritual
nurture and renewal. How prophetic he has been, and how promptly and mirac-
ulously the wherewithal appeared to transform this dream into reality!

Early in 1998 we held a nationwide consultation at East Liberty to focus on
envisioning our new spiritual life center. Prominent leaders in this field from
across the country joined our members, lay leaders, staff, and local professionals in the task. By April of that year a proposal to establish the Cathedral of
Hope Soul Center was presented and approved by session along with the recommendation of an individual to serve as the center's part-time director.

The director of our new Soul Center would be another recent Ph.D. graduate of the Duquesne University program in spiritual formation and a former
Roman Catholic nun. In the coming months, she guided her new spiritual life
committee of session to the formation of a mission statement for the Soul
Center. The statement affirms the center's rooting in the Judeo-Christian heritage and in the Reformed tradition. It speaks of drawing on the traditional spiritual disciplines and "tested spiritual guidance." It proclaims an intention to
honor diversity and to be a resource both to East Liberty Church and to the
whole metropolitan area.

Other Good News

In 1996 East Liberty Presbyterian Church received our denomination's
annual ecumenical service award. The award was given in recognition of our
strong support of the community outreach projects of East End Cooperative
Ministries; our participation in the ecumenical work of the Sister Parish organization that links us with a rural Roman Catholic congregation in Guatemala;
our development of ecumenical relationships through our Taizé prayer service;
and the ecumenical makeup of our church staff.

Also in 1996, the session voted to approve the investment of $500,000 of our
endowment funds in the work of the Ecumenical Development Cooperative
Society (since renamed Oikocredit), a worldwide organization that provides
loans for grassroots, small-business start-ups in the third world. East Liberty's
investment is the largest ever made by a single congregation in the history of
Oikocredit, so news of this commitment landed our church a laudatory editorial

and a front-page story in the *Pittsburgh Post-Gazette*, together with news reports and favorable mentions in several national and international publications.

In our worship, music, and arts department, the good news is that we are now faithfully fulfilling the vision for worship, music, and the arts set forth in our strategic plan five years earlier. The envisioned integration of worship, spirituality, and the arts has flourished under the guidance of our energetic, visionary staff. Our director of music and the arts has initiated a highly successful artists-in-residence program that encompasses about a dozen arts organizations and individual artists, covering a wide spectrum of the visual and performing arts. Our congregational life has been immensely enriched by this truly multicultural, intergenerational, participatory hands-on program.

16

Basement Treasure I:
Bloom Where You're Planted

Back to the Future

In this chapter and the next we will look back at that basement discovery mentioned in the Introduction—the undergraduate research paper I wrote way back in 1958—"The Church in the Changing City," a study of how inner-city churches can survive and thrive. There were, you may recall, six major points derived from the then-current urban church literature of the 1940s and 1950s. Our aim will be to explore the relevance of these points in our experience at East Liberty Presbyterian Church over the past decade as well as to reflect on their broader application for mainline churches in general. Here we will explore the first three of these six points. The second three will be taken up in the next chapter.

Our six points may be summarized as follows:

1. Embracing the potential for becoming a diverse and inclusive congregation.
2. Adapting worship and music styles to the local culture.
3. Extending the church's outreach through advertising and promotion in the mass media.
4. Being actively involved with the church's immediate neighborhood through cooperative, ecumenical mission outreach and community development work.
5. Offering holistic, seven-day-a-week programming.
6. Offering the lost and the lonely a community of caring and sharing, of solace and healing, of values and visions for a purposeful life.

Reaching Out beyond
Racial Cultural Barriers

The Presbyterian Church (U.S.A.), which is currently about 93 percent Caucasian, has officially set a goal for a nationwide membership that will be comprised of 10 percent racial ethnic minority members by 2005 and 20 percent by 2010. An outline of strategies to achieve this goal was adopted in 1998, and printed resource materials were promised by the end of 1999. How is this to happen? How can racially homogenous congregations become more racially ethnically inclusive?

Our own congregation has made great strides in this direction, growing in a decade from 7 percent to nearly 25 percent in our racial ethnic minority make-up. Admittedly, however, we have had several factors working in our favor that most congregations lack. Starting at 7 percent makes it much easier, of course, than starting at 0 percent. Our first African American members joined the church back in the late 1950s, so the next three decades witnessed an exceedingly gradual process of integration. In addition, our congregation's immediate neighborhood has become increasingly African American over several decades—60 percent as of the 1990 census, probably a higher percentage now. That obviously makes the task much easier and more natural for us than for congregations located at some distance from populations of a different racial ethnic composition.

I am quite convinced, however, that even in our situation we would not have experienced anything near the progress we have made over the past decade without having been quite intentional in reaching out to African Americans. A report to our 1998 General Assembly, "Racial Ethnic/Immigrant Evangelism and Church Growth," stated: "The reality is that a predominantly Anglo, Suburban, and Middle Class denomination like the Presbyterian Church must be *very intentional* in its planning and in providing resources if it is going to seriously attract a more diverse membership." First we have to *want* to do it. Then we have to *try* to do it. In our situation, anyway, we have found that where there is a will there is a way.

One does observe that there are many white, mainline congregations located within or near neighborhoods with significant minority populations that are making virtually no efforts to integrate their memberships. In urban areas they may draw their members from a distance. As a result they exist as little, white, suburban "ghettos," isolated from their much more diverse surroundings. While such congregations may have community outreach programs that draw children of different racial ethnic groups into their facilities for after-school programs, tutoring, and so on, they are doing little or nothing to invite these children or their parents to participate in their worship life or in other church programs. When pressed on the point, pastors and lay leaders may rationalize, "Well, they probably have their own churches to attend, and, besides, they wouldn't feel comfortable here anyway." But why should we be hesitant to extend frequent, warm invitations to those regularly coming through our church doors to partic- ipate more fully in the life of our congregations, *provided those persons do not have another church of their own*? Why shouldn't we be doing everything we can to make them comfortable?

Other congregations, wherever they are located, can do the same things we have done. The results, of course, cannot be guaranteed, but here are just a few of the ways in which any congregation can send some clear messages:

1. Establish a partnership with another congregation of a differ- ent racial ethnic makeup than your own.
2. Engage in joint projects, social events, special worship ser- vices, and so on.
3. Invite guest preachers and/or pulpit exchanges with pastors of another racial ethnic group.
4. Welcome guest choirs and/or choir exchanges.
5. Observe the days and seasons special to another racial ethnic group, e.g., a Martin Luther King Jr. Sunday observance, Black History Month, Cinco de Mayo, and so on.
6. Introduce cultural variety into your church music, particularly, of course, the music of the population or populations you want to reach.
7. Find ways to support the causes of another racial ethnic group: helping to promote an NAACP membership drive, passing petitions for a civilian police review board, and so on.
8. Offer courses on the history and heroes, traditions and wisdom of another culture.
9. Seek out racial ethnic candidates when there are openings on your church staff.
10. Plan special events that will interest and attract the racial eth- nic groups you want to reach, then advertise and announce your church events in the community newspapers and publica- tions that circulate among that population.

Adapting Your Worship and Music Styles

There can be no surer sign of your congregation's desire to reach out for diversity than the willingness to adapt your worship and music styles to the cul- ture of a more diverse audience. Herein, however, is likely to be the rub. Even for those pastors and lay leaders who want to reach out and become more cul- turally inclusive, the obstacles may seem insurmountable. You know, for exam- ple, that your style of worship is unlikely to appeal to a different population, yet you can't envision making the necessary changes without upsetting your present worshipers. Furthermore, your music leadership may be resistant, even downright hostile.

Is it not possible, on the other hand, that many members of your congregation might appreciate greater variety of musical cultures than they are presently being offered? You might try a survey questionnaire to find out. You could be surprised. More than a generation after the height of the civil rights movement, it continues to be observed that 11:00 A.M. on Sunday morning is the most segregated hour of the week for most Americans. Is this by intention, or inertia, or lack of leadership? Why is it that in so many other spheres of life we have become so much more multicultural than we are in our churches? Consider how Americans' food tastes have become internationalized since World War II. Look around you at the food court in your regional mall and you will probably observe an international food festival in progress. Salsa now outsells ketchup in the United States! Isn't it possible that many of your church members might also appreciate a greater degree of variety and choice in your worship and music offerings? And, of course, it need not be of a "fast food" quality either. We can and should cull the very best of all the cultures from which we draw.

Another approach, of course, could be an alternative service—another service at another hour on Sunday morning, or Wednesday evening or Sunday evening—offering styles of worship and music that will appeal to different cultures, either racial ethnic or generational. Perhaps some of your current members who have found your traditional worship and music unsatisfying or the Sunday morning schedule inconvenient might also respond positively to an alternative. This could also give you an opportunity to find different musical leadership if your Sunday morning musicians cannot or will not help. Maybe a music leader from a black church would have Sunday evening free, or a good teenage band could help you start a special service for youth.

Our standards, tastes, and preferences for worship and music are inevitably so conditioned by our social class and culture that it often takes a mighty effort to stand outside ourselves and appreciate our own biases. Why else are most white mainline congregations so comfortable with the use of organs, trumpets, and, occasionally, bagpipes to praise God, yet hesitant when it comes to worshiping with African drums or an electric guitar or a drum set or a sitar?

Mainline denominations, such as Presbyterian and Lutheran and Episcopal, have come out of that branch of the Protestant Reformation sometimes called "the Magisterial Reformation." This term points to political realities of sixteenth-century Europe which were such that the religious persuasion of the magistrate—king or prince or duke—dictated which faith would prevail for the whole of the population under his authority. "Magisterial worship" also seems an apt term for the liturgical and musical cultures of these churches whose fates were so closely linked to the preferences of princes and the cultures of their courts. A church service in this tradition is much like a court ceremony with its emphasis on majesty and transcendence, distance and dignity. God as heavenly Sovereign must be worshiped with appropriately regal music.

The tastes of the ruling classes set the standards that prevail in these Eurocentric, magisterial, establishment-oriented traditions. Anything else is inferior and unworthy. The popular preferences of the masses must be resisted. So it is that many church musicians in prestigious mainline congregations continue to focus on a mission of "elevating" popular tastes. And otherwise "liberal" pastors resist the alternative worship and music styles popular in white evangelical churches because they reject the popular "praise" songs as theologically simplistic and musically inferior. Major segments of the population and their tastes are thus dismissed as unworthy of our serious consideration, largely on the implicit grounds of maintaining the traditional standards of our social status.

In a time when businesses offer their consumers greater and greater choice and variety of products, it continues to confound me that so many of our larger mainline churches with multiple Sunday morning services still believe that they must offer identical formats and styles of worship at each service. Why? So as to keep the congregation unified? Does being unified require being monolithic? Does unity require uniformity? Isn't *E pluribus unum* our national motto—"one out of many"? Doesn't the image of the church as the body of Christ suggest that our variety, our diversity, is the very stuff out of which the Holy Spirit makes us one? Can't we celebrate our differing gifts and differing tastes with as much gusto at church as we do at the various ethnic restaurants we frequent?

I remember when I returned from my first visit to the Joy Academy of Church Growth in Phoenix, that I was still pondering how their virtually exclusive focus on one homogenous market segment—young, white, secular, middle-class families—might be translated into our much more multicultural identity at East Liberty. At about that same time, an article in the business section of the *New York Times* caught my eye. It was about the declining market share of ginger ale within total soft drink sales. Market research had established, according to the article, that younger generations tended to associate ginger ale with the elderly, and with being sick and/or hospitalized. Manufacturers of ginger ale, the article reported, had begun to make some headway with this problem by introducing ginger ale in a variety of flavors: raspberry- and cranberry-flavored ginger ale, for example. It struck me then that Presbyterianism had become much like traditional ginger ale in the view of younger "consumers." So why not adopt the same solution: Presbyterianism in a variety of worship and music flavors offered at different times throughout the week?

In many parts of the world today, Protestant churches of the magisterial tradition are floundering and foundering, while Pentecostalism is by far the most rapidly growing expression of Christianity worldwide. Why? Perhaps because it is a religion of and for the masses, often the oppressed and dispossessed of the earth. Perhaps because it offers worship experiences that are emotionally expressive and liberating, music that is pulsating and popular, rituals that promise healing and deliverance. Here is no emphasis on staid liturgical dignity and dour distance but the immediate, dynamic experience of intimate contact with the divine presence. Participants *participate*, swept up together in the power of the Holy Spirit. According to one authority on religious developments in Latin America whom I know—who happens to be my son, R. Andrew Chesnut, professor of Latin American history at the University of Houston and author of *Born Again in Brazil*— Catholic and traditional Protestant denominations alike in our Southern hemisphere are beginning to realize that they must "pentecostalize or perish."[1] The rapid growth of Pentecostalism in Latin America is now threatening to sweep away the centuries-old monopoly of the Roman Catholic Church. Perhaps mainline U.S. churches also have some lessons to learn from the phenomenal growth of Pentecostal churches worldwide as well as from the undeniable success of Pentecostal and neocharismatic churches in our own land. This is a subject to which we will return in chapter 18.

None of the outreach efforts we have been advocating here can be undertaken in an elitist, paternalistic, or patronizing spirit as an effort to "elevate the masses." We must be convinced that we have at least as much to gain from diversity and inclusivity as do those we are trying to reach. This has surely been the case with our congregation's outreach to the African American community. We have received as much as, if not more than, we have given. The deep spiritual authenticity of church music that has emerged from the painful black experience in America, together with the spontaneity and joy, the vitality and enthusiasm of worship in the black church—all offer tremendous potential, I believe, for the spiritual revival of our languishing, white, middle-class, mainline churches. Here too may be the avenue for liberal pastors and traditional church musicians who reject white, evangelical praise music to begin embracing an alternative musical culture that possesses a cultural and spiritual authenticity that is beyond doubt.

One final word about the entrenched insistence that I often find in my own tradition that our worship must always be, first and foremost, "Reformed." I find that this most often means worship that is wordy and left-brained with a fixated and exclusive focus on the First Person of the Holy Trinity. Our worship is strong on the "immortal, invisible, God only wise, in light inaccessible hid from our eyes." But we often overlook "what a friend we have in Jesus" as an equal theme. We neglect the intimate communion into which we are invited both with Jesus as friend and brother and with the Spirit in whom "we live and move and have our being" (Acts 17:28), who is "nearer than breathing, closer than hands and feet."[2] Where is our Trinitarian faith in our worship? Where in our worship do we experience the Christ who dwells within us and among us? Where are the exuberance and joy and spontaneity of the Pentecostal Spirit? It seems we have only heard Paul's admonition to do all things "decently and in order" (1 Cor. 14:40) but ignored his injunction, "Do not quench the Spirit" (1 Thess. 5:19). Maybe we ought more seriously to consider what it would mean to apply our "always reforming" watchword to our worship traditions.

Advertising and Marketing

Until very recently, prestigious professions and elite institutions, including mainline churches, have scorned advertising as crass commercialism beneath their dignity. Aside from a traditional, discreet listing of service hours and sermon topics on the religion page of the local paper, elite congregations would no more think of an advertising campaign than would an elite country club. In marketplace terms, this reflects a carryover from our monopolistic origins in the sixteenth century when some of our mainline denominations were the official, established state churches of the realm. From this viewpoint, it is distasteful and demeaning to think that churches should have to get out there in the open market and scramble for members along with all those other entrepreneurial churches on the fringes of society. *Therefore*, the very act of advertising your church can be a public declaration that you are trying to reach out beyond your present constituency.

Much depends, of course, where you advertise, what you advertise, and how you advertise. If yours is a largely white, upper-middle-class congregation, advertising your church-sponsored classical music concert on your local FM classical music station is obviously not the same bold statement of outreach as advertising a gospel music concert in your local black community newspaper or black gospel radio station.

Strategizing about what, where, and how to advertise is the point where we start to move beyond mere advertising to marketing. Marketing means having a plan that identifies your target audience(s) and includes researched input concerning the most effective media channels as well as the right advertising content and style for reaching your chosen audience(s). When we, East Liberty Church together with a local community theater, cosponsored a concert in our sanctuary featuring the Paul Winter Consort and Bela Fleck and the Flecktones, the event was promoted over Pittsburgh's NPR/jazz FM radio station and in *In Pittsburgh,* our city's free entertainment weekly that reaches an urban young adult audience. When, with the same community theater, we cosponsored a Winans Family Gospel Singers concert, the advertising ran on Pittsburgh's gospel music radio station and in the region's African American newspaper, *The New Pittsburgh Courier.*

Your church advertising efforts need not be expensive, need not involve the costly services of an advertising agency. Current books and workshops can give you plenty of how-to guidance. Not to miss your target, however, you must make sure to consult with and to involve in your planning representatives of those group(s) you want to reach. Then, when you are ready to advertise, flyers and posters can be displayed in store windows and on utility poles. Public service announcements on local radio stations and religious news in local papers are free. Advertising rates in community weeklies are typically very reasonable. Other congregations in your community may carry announcements of certain of your special events in their newsletters and worship bulletins. The best free media of effective promotion, of course, are your members' willingness to invite friends and neighbors to their church together with the word-of-mouth enthusiasm that spreads about a congregation where exciting, significant things are happening.

Special events such as concerts, well-known guest speakers and workshop leaders can pay for themselves with an appropriate admission charge. Other "special events," costing little or nothing beyond some flyers and press releases, may serve more than one purpose—simultaneously drawing media attention, reaching out to unchurched people, encouraging spiritual discipline, and engaging in social action and witness. How about, for example, a campaign to oppose guns and violence by inviting people to join you in a season of prayer, fasting, and marching in the streets?

Many mainline church leaders reject the whole notion of church marketing not only as crass commercialization but also as a capitulation to our free-enterprise culture that encourages churches to promote themselves as if they were selling a commodity. Even worse, they warn, we may be tempted to design that commodity in ways that pander to whatever may be the needs, tastes, and preferences of today's "religious consumers." This is a well-founded concern, of course, a hazard against which we must always be on guard, namely, a temptation to "sell out" for success that has churches competing with one another in a mass media popularity contest. One sure test to determine whether or not we are succumbing to such temptation is to ask, "Are we also willing to stand for certain principles that are not universally popular but that are, nevertheless, right?" Openly welcoming everyone without regard to race, class, or sexual orientation, advocating for gun control, for example, will obviously not "sell" very well to some people either inside or outside the church.

From a positive perspective, we have already seen how marketing can provide concepts and methods to turn the attention of churches outward, beyond their current constituencies to generations, cultures, and racial ethnic groups that they have previously failed to reach. Marketing can provide a discipline for listening to and understanding the needs, tastes, preferences of those we have failed to understand and to attract. This is what all the attention is about in those countless books and workshops that aim to help us understand the baby boomers and Generation X. Marketing can help us to enculturate the gospel for those we are trying to reach. What stands in our way of doing so may well be much less a matter of our core theology and much more a matter of our style preferences, preferences that are very often class/culture/race determined. After many years of experience, I am convinced that a marketing approach need not be a sellout, but can be a very effective tool of contemporary, effective, faithful evangelism.

17

Basement Treasure II:
Mission at Our Doorstep

Partners in Community Mission

Not long after I began my ministry at East Liberty Presbyterian Church, the pastor of a neighboring church invited me to lunch. His congregation, located in a much more upscale neighborhood, was virtually all-white and middle- to upper-middle class, but also struggling with a long membership decline. One of the first things he said to me was, "I envy you your location. Your mission is at your doorstep. Your reason for being is clear. Ours is not." I suggested that we could remedy that by merging our two congregations, selling their building and locating in ours. He seemed interested in pursuing the possibility, but anytime I raised the issue thereafter he was noncommittal. Meanwhile, that congregation continues its slow but steady decline.

That pastor had it right the first time: location, location, location. It might seem strange to apply that real estate mantra to an economically distressed inner-city neighborhood, but to have your mission at your doorstep *is*, indeed, a great advantage for a congregation willing to see it as such. While ten years ago not everyone at East Liberty did see it, by now this view has become virtually unanimous among our leaders and our members. Precisely because we are located at the heart of a disadvantaged community, we are in a position to offer direct, tangible assistance to people in need through a daily lunch program, a men's homeless shelter, an after-school tutoring program, a food pantry, our Family Enrichment Center, and Youth Drop-in Center, and so on. Because we do not keep at arm's length the people who are served by these ministries, we have welcomed into our congregation many new members and friends via these points of entry. In addition, because of our outreach to the immediate neighborhood, we have also attracted from throughout the metropolitan area many other new members and friends who are drawn to our church by our active community mission involvement. We appeal to mission-minded people who want to be involved with a congregation that can offer them an abundance of hands-on opportunities for church-based community service.

The reader may recall that many of the outreach programs mentioned above are interfaith ministries that are housed in our facilities but operated and staffed by the East End Cooperative Ministries (EECM), a cooperative of forty-eight Protestant, Catholic, and Jewish congregations. Most of these are city congregations located in Pittsburgh's East End, but a few are suburban churches. Our congregation provides space and utilities for these ministries, free of charge, plus significant financial support, and many volunteers. In turn, EECM partners with other community service organizations in addition to churches. An effective network with community health care facilities provides health care and drug and alcohol rehabilitation services for men in the homeless shelter. Also, EECM operates its own Bridge Housing program that provides a place to live and employment service for those who have successfully "graduated" from the homeless shelter and rehab programs.

Various forms of community partnership have also been developed between East Liberty Church and other community organizations over the years. Shortly before I arrived at the church, the officers had voted to approve a $500,000 "recoverable grant" from East Liberty endowment funds to assist in reclaiming and renovating—in partnership with East Liberty Development, Inc. (ELDI), our local community development corporation—a row of empty, deteriorating commercial buildings across the street from the church. Included among those buildings is an old, abandoned movie theater that was only partially renovated in this project. As this is written, East Liberty Church and ELDI in partnership are proposing to complete the renovation of this facility and to reopen it as a community theater. In developing this proposal we have worked hand in hand with the Pittsburgh Partnership for Neighborhood Development (PPND), a consortium of three major Pittsburgh foundations committed to working together in supporting local neighborhood development. The Pittsburgh Partnership has provided funding for feasibility studies, consultants, and technical advice regarding the theater's future potential. If the theater proposal passes muster, the PPND group and other foundations will be providing the bulk of the funding both for its physical renovation and for the theater's start-up operating costs.

Actually, and providentially we hope, two proposals concerning the theater's future have been moving forward in tandem. As PPND and ELDI were initiating a feasibility study of the facility's potential as a community theater, East Liberty's director of music and the arts was, independently, formulating a funding proposal for the development of a church-sponsored community arts academy to serve neighborhood children and youth. When the theater feasibility study was completed in mid-1998, it drew the conclusion that the theater project bore promise only if the church's arts academy were to be its major tenant. Now it appears that the two proposals together are synergistically reinforcing one another's potential. As of late 1999, significant foundation funding was being committed to both projects.

Already for several years now, East Liberty has been actively partnering with arts organizations to offer programming for neighborhood children and youth. Much of this was initially developed by our pastoral associate for Taizé and the creative arts. Some of the programming was linked with the weekday, after-school offerings of our Family Resource Center and Youth Drop-in Center, and some of it was offered on Saturdays. After our new director of music and the arts arrived on the scene, he developed an arts scholarship program for community children and youth—a joint project with the Renaissance City Choirs whom he had brought into the church as artists in residence.

Both our East Liberty Church arts initiatives and partnerships and our arts academy and community theater proposals are beginning to look even more promising as part of a larger dynamic of recently emerging, arts-related community renewal efforts. A newly formed, not-for-profit corporation, for example, has recently acquired and renovated a vacant landmark building in our community to offer artists a low-rent residence and gallery space that has been christened "The Spinning Plates Artists Lofts." Following that development, a large artists supply store opened just a block from the church. Even more recently, one of the largest of Pittsburgh's philanthropic foundations has called together representatives of East End arts organizations, with East Liberty included as the one church in the group, to explore how arts organizations can work together to further community development.

Being a Seven-Day-a-Week Church

The same authority on the growth of Pentecostal churches in Latin America that I have previously cited tells me that one of the major competitive advantages that these churches have going for them is that they are always open, always offering services of one sort or another, always there to be of service to those who come for spiritual help. This stands in sharp contrast to the many large, and sometimes prosperous, mainline city churches in this country that during the week, in my observation, stand practically deserted and lifeless. To enter, one must press a buzzer and speak through an intercom. Once inside, one is likely to encounter a secretary or receptionist behind bulletproof glass. Hallways and rooms are dark and quiet as a tomb, the silence broken only perhaps by the quiet murmur coming from a small gathering of elderly women of the church.

Weekdays and weekends, daytime and evening, our Cathedral of Hope is a beehive of activity, functioning in many respects as a full-service community center. Much of what is going on at any given time is our own church programming. Much of it is the activity of the many, many community groups and organizations that utilize our facilities. The happy sounds of children playing, community youth using our gym, retired folks from the neighborhood using our bowling alleys, Family Enrichment Center kids practicing African drumming, and the music of one of the many choirs who rehearse at our church—all mean that our place is very rarely quiet as a tomb.

We believe that both the church and the community groups who use our facilities are benefiting from our relationship. We benefit from the goodwill created by sharing our resources with the larger community in this way. We benefit because just about anytime anyone arrives in our building, the level of activity itself communicates that this is a vital, dynamic, thriving place. We benefit because our colorfully decorated hallways, our many attractively designed posters and announcements of church activities extend a warm welcome to all who use our building to participate fully in the life of our church. Many of our new members and friends do, in fact, come to us through their initial participation in the activities of some community organization or group that meets in our facility. I recently reviewed a list of five dozen such groups that have met regularly or occasionally in our building during the past year.

The traffic in and out of the building day and night contributes to a feeling of greater security in the community surrounding us. We have enhanced this sense of safety by forming our own security staff, composed partially of men who have "graduated" from the homeless shelter and related programs. These dedicated men actually function as a hospitality team, greeting, directing, and assisting people both inside and outside our building, creating much goodwill for the church.

Offering Solace and Support, Healing and Guidance for the Lost and Lonely

The last and the least, the lost and the lonely—that pretty much describes those to whom Jesus reached out with a special concern and compassion. By now the reader can begin to imagine how much of that sort of ministry is going on at our Cathedral of Hope, both through our own ministries and through those programs and services of other organizations using our building. Our Family Enrichment Center has had a special concern for providing practical as well as spiritual and moral support and guidance for families at risk. Arts programs have provided creative personal growth opportunities for inner-city kids who have been increasingly denied such opportunities because the public schools have cut back on their arts curriculum. The holistic and well-networked social services provided for those reached through the homeless shelter and daily meal programs have offered effective tools for the reconstruction of a useful and meaningful life to hundreds of individuals who have lost their way in life.

Lawrence (as we will call him) is a shining example. Here is his story in his own words:

> This is my story of how love brought me back from the dead. On February 24, 1994, I was homeless, jobless, penniless, and spiritually bankrupt. I knew I was addicted to drugs and alcohol, but I was unable to help myself. I could not stop using drugs or alcohol.
>
> Today I know it was God's gentle hand leading me to the EECM Shelter for Homeless Men in East Liberty Presbyterian Church. I lived at the shelter for two months. This is where recovery began with daily attendance at

NA and AA meetings. My will, addictions, and entire life were surrendered to God. With total and unconditional love the shelter staff ministered to me everyday.

After two months "clean" I qualified to enter the EECM Bridge Housing program and stayed there about a year. This program allowed me to seek a deeper relationship with God, pursue recovery, and bridge relationships with family and friends. I enrolled in the Nursing Assistant program at Connelley Technical Institute, graduated and was hired by St. Joseph Nursing Home.

I continued to seek God's plan for my life, worked an honest recovery program and moved into my own apartment. . . . [After another year] God called me to East Liberty Family Health Care Center [as a Nurse Assistant] and the ministry of whole-person health care.

Today Lawrence and his family are reunited. His children have been baptized at East Liberty Presbyterian Church, where Lawrence is an active member and a deacon. He is working hard to give back to others in need what he has himself received, constantly expressing his gratitude to God, to the church, to East End Cooperative Ministries, to all the caring individuals who have helped him along the way.

Finally, let's look at a different sort of human need. Most of our newer gay couples certainly do not fall within the more obvious categories of the last and least, or even the lost and lonely. Many of them are, in fact, among our more "together" members and friends: solid citizens, successful professionals, gifted and responsible individuals, caring and compassionate Christian people. Even such solid individuals as these, however, at times feel the heavy weight of our society's prejudice and discrimination, suspicion and rejection. It is, therefore, all the more incumbent upon the community that professes to follow Jesus to offer such persons a safe haven of respect, support, and encouragement. Because of the social pressures that have pushed gay people away from open, stable, socially accepted, long-term relationships, it is all the more essential that the church morally affirm and spiritually support such relationships. That is why, in my view, the church really ought to be involved in blessing faithful, covenantal, monogamous relationships between same-sex partners as we do between heterosexual couples. I remain saddened that my own denomination, while it officially opposes homophobia and urges us to welcome gays into church membership, also continues to discriminate by denying them opportunities to serve as ordained ministers, elders, or deacons, and by refusing to bless same-sex covenantal unions.

East Liberty Church's most recent show of public support, acceptance, and welcome for gays was our Second Annual Pittsburgh Marathon Sunday Evening Service in May of 1999. Continuing the theme of "Celebrating Diversity" with which we began this special service the previous year, our guest musicians were the Renaissance City Men's Choir and our guest preacher was the Rev. Dr. Mel White. Mel, who had been a faculty member for sixteen years at Fuller Theological Seminary and a ghostwriter for Pat Robertson and Jerry Falwell, came out as gay in late 1991 and published his story in a book entitled *Stranger at the Gate: To Be Gay and Christian in America*.[1] Mel has served as minister for justice of the International Fellowship of Metropolitan Community Churches and now is director of Soul Force. Soul Force, an organization Mel founded, seeks to apply the conciliatory, love-your-enemies principles of Jesus, Mahatma Gandhi, and Martin Luther King Jr. to the struggle for justice and equal rights for gays and lesbians.

In private conversation Mel told me that he had received over one hundred letters containing death threats or wishes or prayers for his death. Many of them, he said, were from ministers! His sermon at East Liberty was poignantly entitled "How Can I Be Sure That God Loves Me Too?" At that same service we publicly welcomed and prayed for faculty, staff, and students from the University of Pittsburgh who were protesting for same-sex partner health benefits for employees of the university.

"I was a stranger and you welcomed me," said Jesus. These are the very first words that appear in Mel White's book telling the story of his own struggle for acceptance and affirmation by the church he has served so faithfully and so long.

18

Learning from the Trends: Past, Present, and Future

Twentieth-Century Trends Foreseen

As we contemplate the need to change—all the many challenges of trans-formation that face mainline churches today—we may very well ask, Are we grappling with the demands of merely temporary fads and fashions or with the pressures of truly enduring trends? I continue to hear some mainline church leaders resisting the contemporary challenges. "If we just wait it out," they say, "the pendulum will swing back in our direction after people tire of the shallow fare of those churches that are booming and thriving today."

The previous two chapters, however, should have answered some of our questions about what is of enduring relevance. The six points of what city churches must do to thrive have remained fairly constant for over half a centu-ry. Further, there is solid additional evidence that some of the other fundamen-tal challenges of change that we face today are of even longer duration.

A century ago, in his magnum opus, *The Social Teaching of the Christian Churches*,[1] German theologian and sociologist Ernst Troeltsch introduced two sociological "ideal types" to conceptualize the primary ways different histori-cal expressions of Christianity have understood and structured their relation-ships within their wider social context: the "church type" and the "sect type."

The church type of Christianity is socially and politically established. It tends to be coextensive with the society in which it exits, so that an individual's national, cultural, and religious identities are more or less inseparable. To be a Serb, for example, is to have ethnic, political, and religious identities that are tightly intertwined. One is born into these identities; they are not chosen. In Western Christian history the church type of Christianity is characteristic both of Roman Catholicism from Constantine up to the modern era and of the Protestant churches that were part of what we have already identified as the Magisterial Reformation, that is, Lutheran, Reformed, and Anglican.

Troeltsch's sect type of Christianity is typical of the early church and of those churches of the Reformation era sometimes called the "left wing of the

Reformation"—Anabaptists such as Mennonites and the Brethren. These churches saw themselves as separated from the larger social, cultural, political realms. They were called out, apart from the world, to focus on the perfection and purity of the Christian life within their small and highly intentional communities. They had no aspirations for influencing the social structures, legal systems, or cultures of the larger world. This is a faith and a way of life that the individual chooses, not one into which he or she is born.

Actually, Troeltsch also identified a third type of Christianity, one that has not been so widely associated with his work, namely, the "mystical type." He saw this type as going back to certain strains within the New Testament itself, and, as he looked into the dawning twentieth century, Troeltsch foresaw this as the emerging type of the future, the one type of Christianity most consistent with the spirit of the modern world. Mystical Christianity has relatively little concern with the social, organizational, institutional structures of traditional religion. This is a much more personalized expression of faith, focused on individual spiritual experiences, freed of the constraints of traditional doctrines and dogmas, tested only by what makes sense to the individual. As with the sect type, individual choice prevails, but unlike the sect type, mystical expressions of Christianity may be purely individual with little or no communal form at all.

P. T. Forsyth, the great British Congregationalist preacher and theologian, also noted the same religious trends that Troeltsch did. While Troeltsch was more the social analyst, Forsyth was a theological critic of the mystical type of spirituality. Writing in 1905 in the preface to his book *The Work of Christ*, Forsyth declaimed:

> We are in a time when a spirituality without positive content seems attractive to many minds. And the numbers may grow of those favouring an undogmatic Christianity which is without apostolic or evangelical substance, but cultivates a certain emulsion of sympathetic mysticism, intuitional belief, and benevolent action. Among lay minds of a devout and impatiently practical habit this is not unlikely to spread. . . . [But] upon undogmatic, undenominational religion no Church can live. With mere spirituality the Church has not much directly to do; it is but a subjective thing; and its favour with many may be but another phase of the uncomprehending popular reverence (not to say superstition) for the recluse religionist, the mysterious ecstatic, and the ascetic pietist.[2]

Forsyth didn't mince words! Whatever opinion Forsyth and Troeltsch held of the mystical type of Christianity, they were right about its rise in the twentieth century. They foresaw the broad outlines of the ascendant spiritual and religious trends of our time, now observed by nearly all those who study such developments. Indeed, whether we like it or not, we must address this religious movement in our own day. One way the great sea change of our time is often expressed is, as we have already noted, "I'm spiritual, but I'm not religious." Translation: "I'm concerned with the quality of my interior life, with the well-being of my soul, with my relationship with the Divine. I'm not interested in organized religion, in denominational distinctions, in traditional rites or rituals, rules or doctrines. I think for myself and I am the one chiefly responsible for the nurture of my soul, for my relationship with the Divine."

Here are some of the outstanding characteristics of the currently widespread spiritual sensibilities in our culture, not just limited to New Agers, that seem to fit with Troeltsch's mystical type and that resonate with many of the same features of "seeker spirituality" and "creation spirituality" that we explored in chapter 8:

1. A focus on individual spiritual experience and freedom of thought rather than inherited religious forms and expressions.
2. A recognition of the validity of a variety of spiritual paths for different individuals at different stages of the journey. An understanding of the spiritual life as a process, as a pilgrimage rather than as a fixed location.
3. A concern for what unites rather than what divides the various great religious traditions of the world, with respect for premodern, preliterate, indigenous religions.
4. A pragmatic test—"you will know them by their fruits"—of the validity of various religious traditions: Do they unite rather than divide people? Do they nurture respect for all traditions and cultures and individuals, and for the earth itself? Do they buttress injustice or champion fairness and equality?
5. A conviction that all persons are the offspring of God, are made in the divine image, and are destined to bear the divine presence within them.
6. A hunger for spiritual experiences that will make a difference, that will heal and transform.
7. Humanitarian and environmental concerns based on a mystical sense of the interconnectedness of all being.

Learning from the Neo-Pentecostals
and Looking to the Future

Two powerful religious trends in America today that seem to be riding the crest of the wave toward the future are New Age spirituality and Pentecostal Christianity. At first, these two movements seem to be at opposite ends of the spiritual spectrum, but in certain respects they both embody major elements of Troeltsch's mystical type of Christianity. Like New Age spirituality, Pentecostal Christianity emphasizes the believer's direct, spiritually transforming experience of God and of divine gifts and powers. There is a relative disregard for the traditional social structures of religion along with an elevation of spiritual gifts and powers above doctrine. There is a valuing of leadership based on natural and charismatic gifts of leadership rather than on institutional or educational credentials.

As we prepare for the next century, mainline Christian churches have much to learn from the revitalization of Pentecostal Christianity in American culture. A very useful contribution to understanding the powerful appeal of neo-Pentecostalism is Donald E. Miller's *Reinventing American Protestantism: Christianity in the New Millennium*.[3] "Neo-Pentecostal" refers to newer churches that emphasize the same traditional gifts of the Holy Spirit as the older, original Pentecostal churches, such as the Assemblies of God and Foursquare Gospel Churches, but have adopted a much more contemporary style.

Miller, a sociologist of religion at the University of Southern California, undertook a five-year research project that included hundreds of interviews together with the extensive use of survey questionnaires completed by pastors and church members. His focus was three neo-Pentecostal movements that originated in Southern California and have since spread rapidly across the United States: Hope Chapel, Calvary Chapel, and the Vineyard Christian Fellowship. These are "new paradigm" congregations—well over a thousand of them in the United States now—that meet in warehouses, sing tunes that would be at home in a nightclub or bar, and have pastors who have never been to seminary. This movement represents, Miller claims, a "second reformation" of Protestantism, and these congregations are, in his view, mediating deeply felt spiritual experiences much more effectively than mainline churches.

So, given the shifting landscape of American religion and the lessons to be learned from the new paradigm churches and the long-term trends previously identified, what can we say about our own future? What will the coming decades be like for mainline urban churches? What challenges will we be facing? I want to name some of the trends I see, drawing here not only on my own insights and the work of Miller, but also on another very useful resource for understanding the big picture of religious and spiritual change in America, present and future: *Shopping for Faith: American Religion in the New Millennium* by Richard Cimino and Don Lattin.[4] Though the authors are principally religious journalists rather than academics, their work has won ringing endorsement from the well-respected sociologist of religion Wade Clark Roof, author of *A Generation of Seekers*.[5]

Here, then, an attempt to glimpse our future:

1. The gap between personal spirituality and institutional religion will grow. Baby boomer alienation from traditional religious institutions will be even more manifest among the population of Generation X. Churches will need to de-emphasize bureaucratic structure, bucking the trend of mainline groups to have endless committees, rules, and regulations. An emphasis on experiencing God's love versus mastering denominational identity and doctrine will continue. Personally transforming

and healing spiritual experience will be of uppermost concern, not denominational loyalty.

2. Spiritual seekers will continue to look to the East for spiritual wisdom and inspiration, and the tendency to blend Eastern and Western spiritualities will grow as Westerners also look more deeply into their own mystical traditions, Celtic spirituality, Gregorian chant, Taizé prayer songs, and contemplative prayer.

3. A blending of the sacred and the secular will continue, including an increasing emphasis on the spirituality of everyday life and "ordinary" spirituality, for example, the spirituality of sex and spirituality and "soul" in the workplace. There will be growing accord between science and spirituality as the search for spiritual truth and for understanding the cosmos converge. Technology and virtual religion over the Internet will increasingly forge links between individuals and religious groups with common concerns. Religious groups and individuals will become more intentional and forceful about extending their influence in society, forging new links between spirituality and social action.

4. Gender specific spiritualities will be developed—different emphases and opportunities will be provided for women and for men. The rising number of women taking up leadership in congregations will change both the style and substance of religion, inspiring a faith that is less rigid and hierarchical.

5. There will be growing appreciation of the connection between spirituality and health by both medical and religious institutions. Spiritual healing is rapidly becoming one of *the* major trends with churches offering anointing, laying on hands, prayer for healing, healing touch. Churches will need to offer "therapeutic" environments, where people feel free to be themselves, to be honest about their vulnerabilities and problems without being judged.

6. There will be increasing emphasis on individual freedom of thought and of choice in matters spiritual and religious, yet individualism will not necessarily undermine the felt need for faith communities, especially new and vibrant ones.

7. More and more churches will take a "market-based" approach to finding and winning new members while displaying more and more flexibility in what they have to offer the unchurched in the way of music, worship styles, programs. Hard-sell evangelism will give way to efforts to meet the unchurched where they are. Growing churches will offer people—in addition to purpose in life—hope, joy ecstasy, and fun!

8. The phenomenon of "mixing and matching," namely, people going to one church for one thing and to another church for something else, will grow.

9. Churches that place high demands on their members morally and spiritually will be the ones more likely to grow. On the other hand, churches will need to put practically no emphasis on fund-raising or high-pressure appeals for money, trusting instead that God will lead people to support mission.

10. More and more congregations will adopt a both/and rather than an either/or stance regarding traditional and innovative worship styles. "Blended" worship styles will prevail. There will be a relaxed, informal air in worship emphasizing the variety in music, casual dress, nontraditional worship spaces, and informal preaching. Churches that evangelize (or advertise) and that offer both "entertaining" and life-transforming spiritual experiences will grow. Holistic expressions of worship, prayer, and meditation that involve the body, senses, and emotions will draw people to labyrinth walking, circle dancing, processions, and the like as they seek a spirituality that is less word- and head-centered.

11. Small groups, especially those where the emphasis is on sharing life experiences and struggles, will continue to be important for people seeking community in a modern society where traditional ties of family and neighborhood are frayed.

12. Leadership will become even more decentralized, with increasing emphasis on lay ministry. Pastoral leadership will empower lay leadership, becoming "trainers" of lay ministers and setting an entrepreneurial, creative, risk-taking, independent, visionary pattern. Traditional denominations will be increasingly decentralized as well, and downsized as more and more emphasis is given to local congregations.

13. There will be a strong congregational emphasis on "unity in diversity." Reaching out to different races and ethnic groups of multicultural America will be a central concern and major challenge for religious institutions. Growing religious pluralism will make denominational identities and boundaries increasingly irrelevant and will inspire fellowship, dialogue, and cooperation between Christians, Jews, Buddhists, Muslims, and other faiths.

14. While "hot button" moral issues will continue to be divisive, there will be renewed efforts to find common ground between religious groups and individuals in conflict over such issues as abortion and gay rights. The religious and spiritual dimensions of environmentalism will be increasingly important since there

is already broad-based lay support for environmental concerns. Congregations will also become more involved in community development and efforts to help the poor.

15. Rationalism will continue to give way to emphasis on dreams, visions, healings, speaking in tongues, and life-transforming experiences of ecstatic joy and profound peace.

16. Mainline churches will need to make room for members who feel a need for deeper experience and commitment without making the "spiritual virtuosi" or the more nominal members feel uncomfortable being in the same congregation with each other.

Cimino and Lattin end their book by saying:

> Strong religious communities with traditional teachings will survive and adapt, particularly those that combine ritual and spirituality. But religious communities that allow the flowering of personal spiritual experience—whether they be Pentecostal congregations or meditation support groups—may enjoy the brightest future. Shopping for faith may . . . threaten the religious powers that be, but this uneasy mixture of practicality and personal faith will mark American religion in the new millennium.[6]

Troeltsch and Forsyth told us as much a century ago. On the brink of a new millennium, the pressing question for our mainline churches—we who for so long grew so comfortable with our "magisterial" status as "the religious powers that be"—is this: How do we respond faithfully and effectively to these persistent trends, both theologically and practically?

19

Evaluating the Trends

Toward Faithful Transformation

In the previous chapter, we explored emerging trends within Protestant Christianity, trends that have accelerated within the twentieth century, trends that are projected to prevail well into the twenty-first century. We have noted how consistent many of these trends are with the characteristics of seeker spirituality and creation spirituality that we explored in chapter 8. In chapter 18 we also set forth point-by-point characteristics of what some well-informed observers of the current religious scene regard as paradigms or gestalts for the "reinvention of American Protestantism," for "religion in the new millennium."

I invite you to reflect on whether or not any of the prevailing spiritual trends and traits of the emerging new paradigm churches and of seeker-creation spirituality may contribute anything to a *faithful* transformation of our old paradigm Protestantism, that is, the major, mainline American denominations. Or, are there such great gaps, both theological and practical, between the emerging "new Protestantism" and the "old Protestantism" that they cannot be bridged without a fundamental loss of our identity, our integrity? Is it simply too great a challenge—as Jesus once suggested in reference to the stresses and strains his transformational ministry came up against when facing old structures, attitudes, and privileges fiercely defended by a resistant religious elite—to put new wine into old wineskins? We have, of course, covered some of this ground already in previous chapters as we have reflected on the challenges of change in such areas as worship, church music, and church marketing. Here we will briefly explore a few other illustrative issues that persistently challenge us today to stretch our old wineskins.

None of our evaluative questions can be answered, of course, apart from our stance within a particular faith perspective, our view from a particular theological vantage point. My own vantage point is that of what I call a progressive, ecumenical, mainline Protestantism. While I will be exploring this mainline orientation and its strengths further in the chapters still to come, space limitations prevent any detailed discussion here of the principal theological foundations of such a faith perspective. For that the reader may want to refer to works such as Shirley Guthrie's long-popular *Christian Doctrine*,[1] or Cokesbury's new adult study series, *Christian Believer*.[2] Again, the best we can offer here is simply some illustrative reflection on certain points at which there might appear to be either irreconcilable differences or promising new possibilities for change and growth as we assess the seeming contrasts between the old and the new of American Protestantism.

One of the clearest of all religious trends, of course, is the rapid erosion of what were once rather hard and fast denominational identities and boundaries. We are well into the "postdenominational era." Congregations of all mainline denominations today are likely to be made up of members who have come from many different denominational backgrounds. These are church members who are less and less patient with any sort of denominational exclusivity or "chauvinism." They want us to focus on what Christians hold in common rather than on what separates them. This does not mean, however, that we must abandon the strong points of our various denominational traditions. In my own Reformed tradition those strengths would certainly include, for example, an intellectually sound and socially transforming faith.

At the same time, the postdenominational trend does challenge us to be open and willing to balance our own strong points with the strengths of other traditions. In the case of the Reformed tradition, for example, that would mean a willingness to appreciate and incorporate the strengths of other traditions that have been more focused on transforming the heart and nurturing the spirit. I am convinced that those congregations that realize, practice, and celebrate their own multidenominational, local ecumenism are themselves already on the transformational path along which contemporary trends are leading us. (As a little aside here, our music director recently led a moving church staff worship service in which the hymns we sang had been chosen to honor the various faith traditions of our staff.) If we are ready to give it more than lip service, this is a path not at all inconsistent with the ecumenism which mainline denominations already profess as one of the essentials of their core identity, namely, that they are but one part of the church universal.

The fact remains, nevertheless, that significant differences of faith and practice do exist between Christians in mainline denominations and congregations. Our current differences, however, have little to do with denominational identity. The factors that unite or divide Protestants today cut across traditional denominational lines. Our differences today have less to do with historical, denominational issues of doctrine and polity and more to do with differing viewpoints on such matters as biblical interpretation and authority, feminism, sexual orientation, abortion, attitudes about mission and evangelism with non-Christian religions, and a progressive or conservative social and political agenda. Broadly speaking, we can identify two principal, but admittedly fluid, "camps" or "wings" into which mainline Protestantism is divided today: the evangelical and the progressive. It is our respective evangelical or progressive perspectives that are more likely to influence our evaluation of contemporary trends, not our traditional denominational differences.

Among the more obvious theological gaps between Miller's new paradigm churches and a progressive Protestant perspective is the Christian exclusivism or particularism of Miller's new paradigm churches, that is, their conviction that all those who have not accepted Jesus as Lord and Savior are lost souls bound for hell. In addition, Miller's study gives us every reason to believe that these same new paradigm churches, though not as biblically rigid as the hard-core fundamentalists, are much more conservative in their approach to biblical interpretation and authority than are progressive mainline Protestants. In this respect, and consequently in the conclusions they draw on such issues as sexual orientation and abortion, the new paradigm churches have much more in common with the evangelical wing of our mainline churches.

Otherwise, I find nothing in the trends of seeker-creation spirituality and of the new paradigm churches that is fundamentally irreconcilable with the essential beliefs and practices of my own progressive mainline Protestantism. This is not to say that there are not some real theological stresses and strains here. Some truly tough challenges are involved, one of which is distinguishing between style and substance in our faith practices. Another is sorting out just how much of what we think is essential to our faith and practice is really determined by our social class and cultural preferences rather than by our core theology. The basic challenge is whether we are willing and able to remain open-minded enough to consider what we might learn from trends that may initially seem foreign to us. Are we able to be pilgrims, to risk drinking from some strange wells rather than adopting a defensive, circle-the-wagons stance toward the changes that are transforming the religious world around us today?

The transformation process we face requires a degree of self-examination, openness, critical thinking, learning, and adapting that will be far from easy for most congregations. Sadly, many will not face the challenges at all, implicitly testifying that they would rather die than change. Also and again sadly, we may simply have to follow Jesus' advice to "let the dead bury the dead." Nevertheless, I draw hope from my own conclusion that there is nothing in the transformational challenges confronting us that would require a repudiation or abandonment of any of our essential beliefs or practices. One important key to the matter is whether or not we are willing to think about these challenges from a both/and rather than an either/or perspective. A prime example, to which we now turn, is how we view the relationship between mysticism and social justice.

Both Mysticism *and* Social Justice

Certainly there are ingredients in the total mix of seeker-creation spirituality and the new paradigm church trends that do not easily fit with mainline

Protestantism as it has been typically formulated and practiced by the various denominations. As we examine some of those areas of belief and practice where mainline Protestantism may find itself most strenuously stretched by the major trends of our time, none stands as more central than the trend toward mysticism and the emphasis on personal, individual spiritual experience.

Mysticism has typically been disparaged by mainline Protestant theologians, as we have heard from P. T. Forsyth nearly a century ago and by many others since him up to the present day. Mysticism has been neither highlighted nor encouraged in the devotion or piety of the typical Protestant congregation. A deep and rich mystical tradition, of course, is to be found in the early desert fathers and in the medieval church, deep wells in the pre-Reformation church from which more and more thirsty Protestants have begun to drink in recent years. At the same time, there are definitely varieties of mystical experience to be found both within the New Testament and within various Protestant traditions. The Gospel of John, the apostle Paul, and John Calvin, for example, each espoused what we might call a "body mysticism," a holy communion of believers with God and with one another through their incorporation into Christ and into his body, the church. By faith and by believing participation in the sacramental, liturgical life of the church, we may become one with Christ as he is one with the Father and the Spirit.

There is also, of course, the "inner light" tradition of the Society of Friends as well as the ecstatic, charismatic mysticism of Pentecostal and neo-Pentecostal Christianity. Protestantism is thus not utterly devoid of any sort of mysticism, though in many instances the various denominational traditions have often lost sight of, neglected, or ignored the mysticism in the Bible and in their own roots. How many Presbyterians, for example, know anything about Calvin's body mysticism or even that he taught the real spiritual presence of Christ in the Eucharist?

Mysticism has typically been criticized by mainline Protestant theologians for its individualism—its focus on "God and me"—and for its alleged preoccupation with the inner spiritual life to the neglect of concern for the community of faith, for neighbors, and for social justice. "Navel gazing" and "pietism" were a couple of favorite slurs employed by my own divinity school professors a generation ago to put down not only mysticism but also any concern with the inner, personal spiritual life. It was also commonly alleged that "mysticism begins in mist and ends in schism."

One need only look to the vital combination of spirituality, community, and social concerns practiced by the Society of Friends, however, to understand that the either/or dichotomizing of spirituality versus community and social justice is utterly unnecessary and often misplaced. As the Quaker author Parker Palmer has put it, the deeper we go into our own connection with the Divine, the more we are aware of our connection with one another, with all life, with all being. Both Thomas Merton and Matthew Fox provide outstanding examples of how the two, mysticism and passion for social justice, may be inextricably intertwined. Robert McAfee Brown's excellent *Spirituality and Liberation* is must reading for anyone who still harbors doubts on this subject.[3]

Both Transcendence *and* Imminence

The challenges of transformation that our mainline churches face today are not just temptations to "get with it" by adapting to the needs and demands of today's "spiritual marketplace," to sell out by offering people whatever sells, to become "the church of what's happening now." The challenges we face are opportunities to learn and grow into a more holistic faith by rediscovering vital dimensions of our own traditions that have heretofore been neglected, ignored, or dismissed.

The fact is, for example, that most mainline Protestant denominations have, until fairly recently, neglected the doctrine of creation. We have assiduously avoided anything that might even hint of "nature worship" or pantheism. We have emphasized the transcendence of the Creator to a degree that we have lost sight of the Creator's presence in the creation. For centuries we failed to teach and preach that we humans are not only called to "subdue the earth," but also to respect, nurture, protect, and defend the integrity of nature as the source of our own life, as the good gift of a good God who has created us too as creatures whose own well-being or shalom is inextricably intertwined with the well-being of the whole creation.

The interconnectedness of all being is a *spiritual* insight and experience deeply embedded in much of the environmental movement and in our own Judeo-Christian traditions. Again, however, the mainline churches have come to this rather late. It was the secular discovery of the environmental crisis that pushed us to this reexamination of our own spiritual tradition. Still, even though we may be late to rally to the cause, by recovering and reaffirming the insight and experience of creation's holy interconnectedness we can realize two important objectives. We can build bridges with one of the most prominent social and ethical movements to emerge within the spiritual ethos of our age. We can also affirm a fuller, more holistic understanding of our own faith tradition.

We need not succumb either to nature worship or to pantheism. But surely we can celebrate and praise the marvelous works of our Creator without mistaking the works for the Creator. Surely we can "see God in all things and all things in God," as Mechthild of Magdeburg put it in describing the moment of her spiritual awakening. This would make us with Paul Tillich and Matthew Fox pan*en*theists, affirming that God is present in all things, not that all things *are* God, which is pantheism. Surely we can also affirm—as did the psalmist and Jesus and Paul and St. Francis of Assisi, and Mechthild, and Hildegard of Bingen, all of our great mystics and most of our foremost classical theologians—that the Creator is revealed in the glory and majesty, the power and beauty of a good natural world that we humans are called to "husband" with the greatest of care.

At our Cathedral of Hope, an annual observance of Earth Sunday in April has become a special, highly anticipated event in our liturgical calendar. In 1999 our 11 A.M. service featured the projection of colored nature slides taken by one of our members, inspirational readings from diverse sources offered by lay people, and a beautiful, ethereal "toning" of Jesus' words, "Behold the Lilies" by Susan Hale. Susan is the author of *Sound and Silence*[4] and a workshop leader at Ghost Ranch, our Presbyterian national conference center in New Mexico. The toning she teaches is typically a spontaneous, "musical," often nonverbal vocalization of one's inner feelings and inspirations that, for some, may approximate the experience of speaking in tongues. Much of Susan's work focuses on toning as a spiritual method for connecting with nature. She joined us at East Liberty Church for Earth Week in 1999 to lead a widely publicized and well-received toning workshop.

Some years our congregation has joined in Earth Week events sponsored by other environmentally concerned organizations. One community-wide Earth Week observance culminated with a Saturday evening concert in our sanctuary. One year we offered a Saturday forum on environmentalism led by a Christian ethicist who then preached for us the next day. Another year our justice and global concerns committee sponsored an adult series on sustainable economic development that eventually contributed to a denominational position paper.

In October of 1998, on the Saturday before the feast of St. Francis, we added to our calendar a brief rite of blessing the animals. Even though it had not been widely promoted, forty-five individuals, many newcomers, showed up with their pets on a cold, rainy afternoon. Three of those newcomers soon thereafter affiliated with our congregation.

Both Universalism *and* Particularism

Is Jesus Christ the only way to God? Is there any sort of balance, any kind of both/and approach possible about this question where the differing views seem to contrast so strongly and clearly between the universalism of seeker-creation spirituality on the one hand and the Christian particularism or exclusiveness of the new paradigm churches on the other hand? A similar divide, of course, often exists between evangelical and progressive mainline Protestants as well. I believe that progressive Protestantism can offer a middle ground here. It is an approach that, admittedly, may not satisfy many on the evangelical side, but I believe it does hold promise for building bridges to the seeker-creation spirituality perspective. It is a position that I would call Christian universalism as opposed to what is often the indiscriminate or relativistic universalism of many New Agers. There is a middle way that does not simply insist that all religions are basically the same, offering equally valid paths to God, but that affirms the particularity, the uniqueness of Christ's person and work without consigning all unconverted adherents of other faiths to eternal damnation.

One line of theological reasoning begins with the Gospel of John's affirmation that the same eternal Word/Wisdom of God that was incarnate in Jesus

Christ was God from the beginning, was in God, and was God's active agent of creation. Thus, the divine Word/Wisdom is structured into the very nature of being itself. Affirming with John that everything that exists was created through the Word/Wisdom of God, we can also affirm that God's eternal Word/Wisdom can then reasonably be expected to appear universally, in other faiths and cultures besides our own. It would then be possible for people of other faiths to affirm and to live by this universal or cosmic Christ presence without ever knowing Jesus the Christ or calling on his name, at least in this life. Of course, as Christians we have the unique standard of the Word of God incarnate in the life and teachings, the death and resurrection of Jesus in order to guide us in identifying that divine presence as it appears elsewhere.

Another approach, in no way incompatible with the one above, focuses on God's redeeming work through Christ. Consistent with the ancient Christian tradition of *Christus Victor*, explored by Lutheran theologian Gustaf Aulén in his influential book by that same title, an *objective* interpretation of Christ's saving death and resurrection holds that the redemption won by Christ is universally applicable to all humankind.[5] Whether they know it or not and believe it or not, all souls are saved. The objective doctrine of salvation developed by Karl Barth, the twentieth century's most prolific and influential Reformed theologian, came so close to implying a universalist conclusion that the issue of whether this is the inevitable outcome of his theology will, most likely, always remain a subject of lively debate.

Christian universalism need not undercut the Christian mission to share Christ with the world, since a whole world of difference for our lives on earth can depend on whether or not we know, believe, and live by this good news, this incredible, amazing grace. Christian faith and life, in this view, can be seen as our calling to "realize" the good news of God's redeeming work in Christ in terms of three meanings of the word "realize": (1) comprehending that redemption as an accomplished reality; (2) by the power of the Holy Spirit to transform our lives, making that redemption real in our own living and in the life of the church; and (3) also by the Spirit's power, living so as to make that redemption real in the world around us.

But what about the last judgment? What about all of the Bible's warnings of hell and damnation? Is this objective view of Christ's redeeming work simply inviting people to have their cake and eat it too, to live this life however they please since they are assured of eternal life in the next? (Of course, the apostle Paul faced this same objection to his doctrine of salvation by grace.) One can certainly reason, as P. T. Forsyth did, that in a very real way the last judgment took place already when Christ died upon the cross, bearing the sins of the world. This is yet another variation on the theme of Christ's work as objective and universal. The cross reveals that the purpose of God in judging our sins is not to destroy us but to redeem us, to deliver us. After all, what loving parent would ever seek to punish or discipline his or her children with any other purpose in mind except to correct them, to set them straight? Certainly no such parent would aim to destroy his or her children, or do them irreparable harm.

We must each, of course, still face our own individual accounting with God. But in the light of the above affirmation we may expect that in the end God's purpose in judging us is to redeem us. Suppose that our own last judgment is something like a comprehensive life review in which we come face to face with the ultimate reality of our attitudes, choices, and behaviors and their impact for good or ill on other souls. This purgative process may well feel exceedingly long and painful for some souls, indeed, like an eternity of struggling to come to terms with ourselves and with God.

In the end, I believe that all souls will come to God through Jesus the Christ. So I can affirm his words in John's Gospel as the words of the Cosmic Christ through whom all souls will come at last to God: "I am the way, and the truth, and the life. No one comes to the Father except through me" (John 14:6). I also believe, as Jesus himself more than once suggested, that there will be some real surprises at the last judgment. Many Christians who thought they knew Jesus and constantly called on his name may find when they meet him face to face that they do not recognize him at all. Others, non-Christians, may also be surprised when they meet him. "Oh, that's who you are," they will say. "I knew you all along. I just didn't know your name."

From perspectives like those suggested above, it is quite possible for Christians to hold to the uniqueness of Christ and his saving work while also engaging in dialogue and cooperative action with people of other faiths in ways that are mutually beneficial and enriching. We Christians can honestly share what we believe and honestly hear what people of other faiths have to share without the burden of feeling that we must convert non-Christians to our faith.

Has it not been one of the curses of human history that people of one faith have believed that they must impose their faith on others, or even worse, have felt justified in oppressing or exterminating others who are branded as "heathen" or "pagan savages"? Considering that our world today is suffering from a frightening revival of various brands of ethnic and religious fanaticism, we might even say that pursuing interfaith dialogue and cooperation is a religious, moral imperative. This is why I am delighted to be involved, and to get our congregation involved with the United Religions Initiative spearheaded by Bishop William Swing of the Diocese of California of the Episcopal Church. Bishop Swing is scheduled as guest preacher at East Liberty's third annual "Celebrate Diversity" Sunday evening service on May 7, 2000, when our focus will be on interfaith understanding and cooperation. We eagerly anticipate a truly interfaith celebration that evening with Bishop Swing sharing his vision for a worldwide organization bringing various faiths together at both the grassroots and at the international levels.

Loving God with *both* Heart and Head, *both* Body *and* Soul

Hungry Hearts is the title of the newsletter published by my own denomination's office of spiritual formation. That office is less than ten years old because, once again, we have been late to recover this ancient tradition from the church universal, and late as well to discover the spiritual hunger so pervasive in our supposedly secular world. Presbyterians have typically been strong on a Christianity that feeds the mind with sound theology. Well and good, but the heart and soul need feeding as well. And it is not necessarily the full-blown mystical experiences of St. John of the Cross, Teresa of Avila, or Julian of Norwich that spiritually hungry souls are seeking today. It may simply be a faith and faith practices that give priority to the spiritual disciplines that nurture a personal relationship with the living God.

For some hungry souls, the soul feast may be found in something like John Wesley's evangelical experience, an experience he described as his heart being "strangely warmed" by the gospel. (This individual evangelical experience, by the way, though it powerfully shaped the spirituality of the Methodist movement, was also combined with a passion for the community of faith and for social justice in the wider world,) For others, the soul food may be provided by what many of our regular Taizé prayer participants profess to be a spiritually refreshing, transporting form of devotion, and also one that is combined with a concern for social justice.

Some souls may satisfy their hunger in the prayerful walking of a labyrinth or in the laying on of hands and anointing with prayers for divine healing. For some it may be found in the personalized study of scripture that is offered in the increasingly popular Ignatian method of *lectio divina*. The spiritual hunger may lead some to meet regularly with a spiritual director/companion/mentor who can help individuals one-on-one to find the presence of God in scripture, in prayer, in dreams, in personal decisions, in daily work, and in relationships. Mind, heart, soul may also be fed by theological and liturgical studies that open the doors of the mind and heart to perceive profound new meaning and power in the body mysticism of the church's sacramental, liturgical life, a mysticism that I believe also has profound social and ethical implications.

Belief in the healing power of prayer and other spiritual practices, long ignored by mainline Protestantism, was long ago affirmed by Christian Scientists, then by the Unity School of Christianity, then by Pentecostal and charismatic Christians, then more recently by spiritual seekers, holistic health practitioners, and now even by many mainstream physicians. Mainline churches, however, are still generally way behind the curve. Why? Admittedly, there is justifiable concern when belief in spiritual healing leads to a rejection of medical science, or when prayer or other spiritual healing methods are approached as magical, or when false guarantees of a cure are held out, or when blame for their illness is placed on those who are suffering for their own supposed lack of sufficient faith. What stands between many mainline congregations today and any vital practice of spiritual healing, however, is not that it is inherently inconsistent with our core theology. Rather, the obstacle is our outdated rationalistic, materialistic Enlightenment worldview that has left no room for divine intervention, for spiritual mysteries, for the miraculous.

While many of the spiritual practices mentioned above are rather new and still unfamiliar to most mainline Protestant congregations, there is nothing in any of them that is inconsistent with our traditional beliefs. In fact, many of them are ancient practices of the church universal and take us back to a more faithful and holistic practice of our faith in a God of transforming presence and power who is active in our daily lives. (Try removing from the New Testament all references to spiritual healing, divine intervention, and the miraculous and see what you have left!) I am convinced that these spiritual practices will grow in those congregations that are responding to the spiritual needs of our age, receptive to God's transforming work.

20

Transforming People, Transforming Organizations

Transforming Leadership

In his study of outstanding leaders in a wide variety of fields, *Leadership*,[1] Warren Bennis concluded that the essential characteristics of effective leadership are (1) to be possessed by a vision, (2) to be able to communicate the vision to others so that they too can see it and claim it, (3) to know one's self well and to be confident of one's strengths, and (4) to endure, to persist in the face of obstacles and opposition.

Daryl R. Conner, author of *Managing at the Speed of Change,* adds another, perhaps as a subpoint under endurance: resiliency.[2] Conner, widely recognized as the world's top change management expert, offers a comprehensive theory and process for managing change. The process requires effective leaders who, first and foremost, are able to nurture in themselves and in those they lead a resiliency that includes the capacity to anticipate change; to expect the unexpected; to adapt, to learn from and bounce back from setbacks; to understand and manage the process of planned change. Conner's change process also entails the recruitment and development of other leaders within the organization who will work as interpreters, agents, and advocates, committed to advancing the cause of change within the organization.

As we have learned already from various sources in the preceding pages, it is visionary, transforming leadership of clergy and laity alike that is the key to transforming our churches. Economist, business consultant, and futurist Harry Dent Jr. states the matter boldly and succinctly in his book, *The Roaring 2000s.* Addressing the radical ways in which business organizations must change in order to succeed in a rapidly changing environment, Dent points to leadership as the key factor: "Visionary individuals, entrepreneurs, and leaders will spearhead this change, not institutions, committees, and bureaucrats."[3] And, again from Dent:

> The best entrepreneurs, executives, and investors I have worked with
> . . . have a clear understanding of change and fundamental trends that

seem all but inevitable to them. They appear risky and unclear only to people who don't understand such changes and naturally cling to familiar patterns that are more comfortable. . . . A clear vision of future change and the discipline to stay the course are the keys. . . . Setbacks are only opportunities to learn, adapt, or invest more.[4]

Peter Senge in his marvelously wise and insightful *The Fifth Discipline: The Art and Practice of the Learning Organization* offers systemic balance to Dent's view of leadership. Senge writes:

> The new view of leadership in learning organizations centers on sub-tler and more important tasks [than simply being "in charge" and, sup-posedly, having all the answers]. In a learning organization, leaders are designers, stewards, and teachers. They are responsible for *building organizations* where people continually expand their capacities to understand complexity, clarify vision, and improve shared mental models—that is, they are responsible for learning.[5]

What a wonderful gift it is that those of us who are pastors are expected by the very nature of our role to lead through learning. We are called to teach and preach, to offer spiritual wisdom and guidance, to point people again and again to a God-given vision and mission for our lives both as individual disciples and as the church of Jesus Christ! What a wonderful gift it is to work and serve within a faith-based organization where mission and vision are the very heart and soul of our enterprise in comparison to business organizations where, for example, the task at hand is manufacturing shoelaces or widgets.

To lead is to have some notion of where you and your organization are going, to stimulate and elicit the development of a communal mission and vision and then to inspire and encourage others to move in that direction together. Leadership requires having a compass, knowing, as Stephen Covey puts it, which way is north. In fact, Covey's *Seven Habits* provide us with won-derfully wise, spiritually based, step-by-step guidance for nurturing and devel-oping both individual and communal or organizational growth. At East Liberty Church we have made extensive and fruitful use of the *Seven Habits* in adult education, sermon series, and leadership training. Covey's theory and Daryl Conner's, by the way, are compatible and complementary. They both lead us in the end toward the goal of developing synergy.

The Path of Personal
and Organizational Transformation

The *Seven Habits* are sequential, developmental. Each step builds on those that precede it. Here is what those habits look like when translated, as I have done below, into the clearly faith-based foundations upon which I believe Covey, a devout and very open-minded Mormon, has developed them:

1. Becoming proactive, nurturing the conviction that God has given you charge of your own (your group's or organization's) life, believing that you are created in God's image, divinely endowed with multiple gifts that God commissions you to develop and utilize for good ends. You are a co-creator with God, co-creator of the world and of your own life.

2. Knowing, clarifying, formulating your (your group's or organization's) God-given purpose in life, your vocation, your mission, your direction. Being clear about where you are going and committing your mission to writing.

3. Putting first things first in your life. Being self-disciplined, a good steward of all your God-given resources, taking charge of the details, the process, the management of the day-to-day practical steps that are necessary to get you (your group or organization) where you're going, to accomplish your mission, to turn your vision into reality.

4. Moving beyond competitive, win-lose attitudes to formulate and pursue win-win solutions. Becoming less self-centered, learning to work with others cooperatively, harmoniously, productively. Finding yourself as you give yourself to others in cooperative endeavors. Believing that as you give, so shall you receive. Having an abundance mentality, believing that life need not be a zero-sum game, that there is plenty of everything to go around.

5. Seeking first to understand, then to be understood. This habit entails developing the attitudes and the communication skills that enable you first to be a good listener, to put yourself in the other person's place, and then to state your own needs and perspectives in ways that encourage others to listen and understand you.

6. Contributing to synergistic group dynamics. In Christian terms this is being able to honor and celebrate our different individual gifts, to give and receive as contributing members of the body of Christ. As Paul portrays it, each member, like an organ in the body, is making his or her own unique contribution to the healthy functioning and upbuilding of the body so that all are growing individually and corporately into the likeness of Christ. Synergistic relationships mean that, in dynamic terms, the whole is greater than the sum of its parts. As Covey puts it, synergy means that two plus two equals more than four, maybe forty, or four hundred.

7. Nurturing a process of continuous personal and professional (as well as group, organizational, and communal) growth and self-renewal. Holistic growth is social, intellectual, spiritual,

emotional, and physical. It requires taking time out to renew yourself (your group or organization) in body, mind, and spirit. It entails continuing education, recreation, meditation, worship and prayer, reflection, mental and physical exertion.

This is all good stuff for us Christians. In fact, I am sometimes amazed by the degree to which many of today's leading business authors draw on biblical and spiritual wisdom, either explicitly or implicitly. Sometimes the secular world surprises us by recovering ancient spiritual wisdom of which our churches have grown neglectful. Peter Senge in his organizational theory, for example, lifts up spiritual elements such as conversion, self-transcendence, compassion, forgiveness, reconciliation, and love! Both Covey and Senge point us back to the roots of our faith and forward to the kind of church organizations and faith communities that the future will increasingly require us to be, namely, churches that promote the comprehensive, holistic growth of their members. Senge and Covey are worth going back to again and again. But let us also remember that Paul got there nearly two thousand years before they did with his notion of the church as the living, growing body of Christ in which the dynamics of continuous personal and group growth are intertwined, nurturing us all to maturity both individually and collectively into the very likeness of Christ.

Harry Dent sees a future already here in which the course of human development will make it increasingly the norm for individuals to pursue a path of personal growth their whole life long. We will become ever more proactive and self-actualizing, working within organizations that grant us more and more self-direction and space for creative thinking and experimentation, less and less bound by organizational rules and regulations.

> As our life expectancies increase, and as our education and human development stretches later into life, we develop higher capacities for complex consciousness. . . .That's why we must stop trying to recreate the past. There is no going back in the evolution of consciousness, intelligence, and the educational systems that cultivate them. Instead, we must go forward to the next stage, and start bringing new principles into our institutions and business organizations.[6]

Church research consultant and author Mike Regele sees an emerging global consciousness of which churches must take serious note.[7] In spite of certain world events that might suggest otherwise, people everywhere are becoming more and more aware of the larger world, of other cultures and other faiths. They are less and less satisfied with either absolutistic or relativistic thinking. They want to identify and claim the core values and virtues that, across all our differences, hold us together as a human family.

This view is certainly compatible with James W. Fowler's work on stages of faith development. Fowler identifies the final, most mature stage as one of a "universalizing faith."[8] A universalizing faith has probed to the depths of its own particular tradition and is thus able to recognize that depth in other traditions. Exemplars of this stage of faith are Mahatma Gandhi, Martin Luther King Jr., Mother Teresa, Dietrich Bonhoeffer, Abraham Heschel, Thomas Merton. Leaders who have reached the stage of universalizing faith may well be prophets and reformers. Out of the greater unity they envision, they are often led to challenge, reform, and sometimes overthrow the conventional rules, doctrines, and institutions of their own particular traditions. For this they must often pay a heavy price, offering even the ultimate sacrifice of life itself. Thus to the qualities of outstanding leadership indicated above, we must add an additional subpoint under endurance: courage.

The Shape of Organizational Transformation

Harry Dent declares:

> I have found that structure determines behavior. Changing the structure
> of an organization, including measurements and rewards, is the only
> way to establish genuinely new behavior. The secret to corporate
> change is that you must shake up the old system and create a new struc-
> ture first.[9]

Well . . . maybe. I have seen my own denomination go through a whole series of structural changes over the past twenty-five years or so, and right up to the present day, without experiencing much true renewal or transformation in the process. The reader will also be aware by now that any really significant structural change at East Liberty Presbyterian Church was not accomplished until the eighth year of my ministry. In the meantime, nevertheless, many significant changes were accomplished in other areas of church life—sometimes by just going around the system, sometimes through slow but persistent work to reshape congregational culture.

Senge, however, says something very similar to Dent on this subject: "It is fruitless to be the leader in an organization that is poorly designed."[10] For my part, I will concede this much to Dent and Senge: If we had succeeded much earlier in our efforts to make structural change at ELPC, other changes could have been made sooner and with less resistance and conflict. At the same time, I would say that transforming organizational cultures and subcultures is just as important as, if not more important than, redesigning the organizational structure, though both structure and culture are, of course, closely intertwined.

Dent works from a theory of cyclical change, cycles of interrelated social, economic, and cultural change that, in the modern world, have been brought about by the emergence of new economies every eighty years or so. Invention, innovation, experimentation, and risk taking characterize the ethos of that phase of the cycle in which a new economic reality is emerging: the industrial revolution, for example, then the assembly line, then the computer. Each of these innovative phases, during which productivity receives a major boost, is followed by a phase in which the emphasis is on organizing, consolidating, and institutionalizing the changes introduced in the previous phase. We are now in a period of major change brought about by the introduction of the computer and computer networks. This is reshaping not only production but also the way we organize, hence, the emerging network model of organization.

These alternating cycles of change and consolidation account for much of the resistance and conflict that are experienced within organizations and institutions and between one generation and another. Those persons reared in the culture of one generation may find themselves as adults living within a new ethos of very different values and demands. Today, older adults who were shaped by the assembly line ethos of institutional loyalty, obedience to authority, top-down control, adherence to rules and regulations, and "coloring within the lines," now find those values overturned, rejected, and discarded as we enter the era of organizational networks. This often makes the challenge of change difficult and filled with conflict because what the present and future require is individual creativity, innovation, risk taking, and the willingness to think for one's self.

What the present and future require, in Dent's view, is a network organizational model in which leadership is from the center rather than top-down; front-line teams are empowered to customize solutions; bureaucracy is eliminated; and an entrepreneurial spirit prevails *within* the organization.

Transforming the Church Organization

Translating some of these organizational perspectives into recommendations for mainline church organizations leads us in the following directions:

1. Effective church organizations must work to eliminate all the unnecessary bureaucracy and red tape that complicate and prolong decision-making processes. Ministry and mission must be the priority, not, in Dent's words, "red tape, petty power plays, and emotional problems."

2. We must foster a congregational culture climate in which creativity, innovation, experimentation, teamwork, and risk taking are encouraged, supported, and rewarded. Encourage brainstorming and "can-do" attitudes among leaders rather than knee-jerk, gatekeeping and faultfinding responses when new proposals or solutions are advanced.

3. Boards and committees must delegate more decision-making authority and responsibility to those on the front line (staff, lay ministers, ministry teams) so that the front line can respond quickly and effectively to the needs of the individuals they are serving. Clarify their authority and responsibility vis-à-vis committees and boards, and evaluate results.

4. Most standing committees should organize ministry teams under their direction to whom are delegated ongoing, routine tasks with as much discretionary authority as reasonable. This will free committees to focus more on the big picture while offering hands-on service opportunities for those who enjoy working for a period of time on certain tasks of a fairly limited scope. For example, under the worship, music and arts committee there might be an array of teams on ushering, greeting, Communion preparation and serving, sacristy, seasonal decorations, and so on.

5. We must provide many hands-on opportunities for lay ministry (e.g., the Stephen ministry programs) for baby boomers and younger generations who are generally much less interested in serving on church boards and committees than are older generations.

6. We should help members to identify, assess, develop, and utilize their gifts for hands-on ministry and service. This will greatly increase the corps of those offering frontline service for the church. This means training, trusting, recognizing, and empowering lay ministry.

7. Staff, lay leaders, and standing committees must focus on the big picture. This means enabling staff and lay leaders to function at a higher level that emphasizes visioning, setting goals and priorities, evaluating, not micromanaging programs and projects.

8. Most church boards and standing committees should meet no more often than every other month, possibly quarterly, but for a longer period of time at each gathering. A quarterly meeting—which might be held on a Saturday from 9:00 A.M. to 4:00 P.M. rather than for two or three hours on a weekday evening when people are often tired following a day's work—should focus much less on routine business and much more on visioning, worship and spiritual nurture, relationship building, continuing education, brainstorming, goal and priority setting, and evaluating.

9. Terms of service on church boards, committees, ministry teams, and other church organizations should be limited by a pattern of regular rotation of members on and off these bodies. This will assure more opportunities for all to serve, especially young adults, and will give the church organization a refreshing inflow of new people with fresh ideas. It is especially important to recruit representatives of younger generations and to provide leadership training that will assist them to develop their potential.

The Path of Transformation:
Revolutionary or Evolutionary?

Developmental models for personal and group growth assume an incremental, evolutionary process of change. We know as well, however, that change sometimes can be or must be sudden, dramatic, revolutionary. After all, death and rebirth are the fundamental path of Christian faith and life. A spiritually based Christian paradigm of change will recognize both paths as valid depending on the situation. There is a process of spiritual change that centers on repentance and conversion, and another that focuses on an incremental process of development, of learning and growing. Generally speaking, both paths are equally valid spiritual dynamics of Christian faith and life. Each individual and every group will probably experience both, perhaps sequentially, perhaps simultaneously. Which path we take may well depend on our goals and our circumstances, and on the crises and challenges we face. Over the past decade at East Liberty Church we have, I believe, affirmed and pursued both of these paths as we have journeyed toward bringing our vision into reality.

There are authorities in the field of business who reason that ours is a time of such radical and fast-paced change that nothing will do for business organizations but radical change. "These times," declares Dent, "demand revolutionary change, not simple evolution. [They demand leaders] who have the courage and foresight to lead the way."[11]

Both Dent and Conner affirm what I had intuited from the beginning of my ministry at East Liberty: Sometimes a threat to our survival can be the most effective impetus to change. Because most of us are much more comfortable with what is familiar rather than what is unknown, and because maintaining the status quo seems much less risky, most of us—including leaders—are resistant to change. Often it is only a sense of life-or-death urgency that can propel us toward accepting and implementing significant change. Dent writes:

> Whatever the cause, urgency works to eliminate the natural human resistance to change. It is a true luxury for a change-oriented leader or project team, because most people will face reality more directly, react less selfishly, and exhibit heroic efforts when faced with a truly urgent situation. You can leverage such an urgent situation to make rapid changes in a matter of months that, in a relatively successful and stable organization, may take years.[12]

It is also true, however, that if we do succeed in successfully leveraging change with a sense of life-or-death urgency about the organization's survival, we will very possibly then face a new challenge. With their sense of urgency now diminished by success, people within the organization may then be tempted to return to their old ways of infighting and turf wars. To a certain extent, this explains what happened to East Liberty in 1994–95. Things were then looking so much more secure than they had five years earlier, that certain individuals and organizations in the church felt more comfortable about taking up their internal cudgels with a renewed vigor.

When an organization is not in crisis mode we can turn to Senge and Conner to help us understand and move forward through a process of planned change and continuous transformation. Dent suggests that when we do not have the leverage of life-or-death urgency, the better way to introduce significant change is through the pilot-project approach. This method too has worked for us at East Liberty Church. Initially, for example, rather than trying to introduce major change in the 11:00 A.M. worship service, we experimented with other services at other times of the week with a commitment to evaluating them after a clearly stated period of time.

This approach has worked well for us with another of Dent's recommendations, namely, to develop, encourage, and give lots of latitude to small frontline teams who know the needs of the "customers," and to empower those teams to experiment with new and better ways to meet customer needs. This is precisely what we have done with our Sunday night WorldBeat Spirit Party experiment, held away from the church in a popular club—reach out to young adults. We entrusted its development and execution to two younger staff members who are ages twenty-something and early thirty-something and who understand the age group we're trying to reach.

21

What Is the Hope
for Mainline Churches?

First, the Bad News

Sociologists of religion Roger Finke and Rodney Stark make a convincing case in their work *The Churching of America, 1776–1990: Winners and Losers in Our Religious Economy*[1] that the decline of mainline churches relative to the total U.S. population is nothing new. Indeed, their impressive array of facts and figures and their mastery of the relevant literature point to a decline that has been under way since colonial days. Supporting the earlier thesis of Dean Kelley's *Why Conservative Churches Are Growing*,[2] now over twenty-five years old, Finke and Stark argue that the primary dynamic at work is the lessening demands that churches make upon their members once they become established and comfortable. The higher standards, the strictures and stringencies of emerging sect-type churches give them a decided advantage. While the mainline churches are accommodating to the world and progressively weighed down with freeloaders and deadwood on their membership roles, the sect-type groups are increasingly strengthened by members who have zealously committed themselves and their resources to the faith, passionately determined to win new recruits to it.

As if this were not enough bad news, then comes Mike Regele with his carefully researched assessment of the future prospects for mainline churches. Regele is cofounder and president of Percept Group, Inc., a California-based marketing information company focused on providing churches with demographic data and extensive survey information about values and religious attitudes in the communities they serve. The Percept group has worked with close to thirty thousand congregations in the United States, helping them to understand their cultural context and to formulate new visions in the midst of rapid social and cultural change.

In his book *The Death of the Church*, Regele admits to being a moderate Presbyterian who loves the Presbyterian and Reformed heritage. Still, he must tell it like it is, warning mainline churches of the involuntary death they are facing unless they voluntarily die to what is past, as Jesus enjoined us, in order to be reborn to a new future of promise. The church, he says, has a choice: to die as a result of its resistance to change or to die in order to live. "If we choose to follow the status quo strategy, the church as we have known it will be crushed in the seismic waves of change that are rattling our lives."[3]

Among the life-threatening challenges facing us in Regele's analysis are these:

1. Mainline churches are overwhelmingly white, but racial ethnic minority populations are growing while the white percentage of U.S. population is projected to decline from close to 80 percent in 1990 to only a little over 50 percent in 2050.

2. The white population is growing older and with a declining birthrate, but the nonwhite populations are of a much younger average age with a much higher birthrate. This places the mainline churches in the predicament of having an increasingly elderly membership entrenched in Eurocentric traditions of church culture while the rising generations are more and more multicultural. "While most of us find it difficult to see the difference between the Gospel and our Presbyterianism, other cultures can."[4]

3. Generational cultural differences have worked against us because our mainline churches have had, for many years now, a predominance of members and leaders drawn from the two pre-boomer generations: the "builders" (born between and 1901 and 1924) and the "silent" (born between 1925 and 1942). These generations have difficulty understanding the boomers, their values and their worldviews. They often resent the changes in the world around them, their own diminishing power and influence, so they act as obstructionists, digging in their heels in the face of change.

4. The silent have felt caught between the generations that preceded and followed them. For some this produces angst and anger that can result in "a growing stubbornness" and "progress blocking behaviors."[5] On the other hand, there are significant numbers of silents who have gone the other way and thrown their lot with the boomers. (By the way, according to Regele, this is why there was such a widespread, emerging new interest in psychotherapy in the 1960s. A great number of those in the silent generation were trying to work through their identity in relation to whether they should take the path of the builder generation that preceded them or that of the baby boomer generation that followed them. That certainly resonates with my life history.)

5. Boomers are visionary, idealistic, more inner-directed and big-picture oriented, impatient with the institutional busywork, hierarchical organization, petty power plays, obstructionist gatekeepers, and bureaucratic red tape that characterize so many mainline congregations.

6. Current patterns of religious affiliation and preference favor the more conservative churches, but they too can be expected to struggle against overall trends of *dis*affiliation and weakening loyalty that point to an American society in which only about one-half the population has any level of active faith by around 2013.

7. Our mainline seminaries are not preparing visionary spiritual leaders who can cope effectively with the new social and cultural realities.

From my own observations, I would have to agree that we are failing miserably in attracting and developing the kind of ministerial leadership we need to guide us through the transformational process that our mainline churches require if they are to survive and thrive in the new millennium. With some exceptions, of course, our seminary faculties are good at steeping their students in tradition but not in fostering any spirit of creativity, any visionary, innovative leadership, or even much curiosity about the new world in which they will be ministering. In addition, the dynamics of academic specialization push students toward false dichotomies rather than toward synthesis and synergy, that is, spirituality vs. social justice, liturgics vs. ethics, and so on, thus making it difficult for seminarians to put it all together in any kind of vision of holistic ministry.

Though he writes for a business audience, Harry Dent has articulated a vision of transformational leadership that we must have, yet for the most part do not have within many of our seminaries, congregations, or denominations. It is a vision of

> dynamic organizations . . . fueled by leaders at all levels, that can attract the best talent, and motivate them to higher levels of performance instead of merely following the rules of the past era. We must create attractive causes and learning environments that draw the best people and cultivate their inner spirit for growth and success.[6]

Just one more quote from Dent that I cannot resist because it speaks so well to the leadership we need from both clergy and laity:

> Proactive, self-actualizing people give the system its cause—its direction and focus, consistent with the objectives of the organization as a whole—through constant innovation, communication, and creative decision making. People throughout the organization must be trusted to make good decisions and must be rewarded for taking risks. They need

the skills, expertise, and information to choose intelligently. But, most important, they must understand the organization's vision.[7]

Now for Some Good News, Maybe

What is the prophetic word from the Lord for mainline churches? Is it the warning from Jeremiah, "For thus says the LORD: Your hurt is incurable, your wound is grievous. There is no one to uphold your cause, no medicine for your wound, no healing for you" (Jer. 30:12–13)? Or is it the promise, also from Jeremiah, "For surely I know the plans I have for you, says the LORD, plans for your welfare and not for harm, to give you a future with hope"(Jer. 29:11)?

The issue will be settled, of course, congregation by congregation. But all is not lost. The news in Regele's analysis is not entirely bleak, though sometimes it is necessary to read between the lines to find the glimmers of hope. Also, in some instances I have translated his warnings into promises in the points that follow. It must also be said again and again, however, that the glimmers of hope here will come as good news only for those congregations that are willing to read and heed the signs of the times. A number of these factors, if properly understood and taken advantage of, should give a decided edge to progressive mainline churches. There *is* hope for congregations that are willing and able to engage these challenges constructively by:

1. Clarifying and claiming their identity, mission, and vision, reaching out enthusiastically to share with others the gospel message of deliverance, of hope, of new and abundant life offered in God's love incarnate in Jesus of Nazareth and then embodied anew in the life of Christ's church.

2. Understanding that the development of consciousness in our postmodern period gives an advantage to religious communities that are neither absolutistic nor relativistic in their approach to religious truth. Postmodern people increasingly realize that they have choices among various worldviews. They do not expect to be told what or how to think or believe. They expect, rather, to be active participants in a dialogical process by which the "social construction" of religious reality takes place in their chosen faith community. They expect to be listened to rather than talked at by their spiritual leaders to whom they will offer no respect or deference simply on the basis of their office or rank.

3. Responding positively to the concerted new efforts emerging—consistent with an intellectual position that is neither absolutistic nor relativistic—to identify a new common ground across cultures and belief systems. There is a new worldwide consciousness developing that "will have a distinctly global

perspective with a high level of cultural inclusiveness. The rise of globalism will make this inevitable."[8] Globalism fosters a quest for universally shared moral values to which all civilizations subscribe and without which no civilization can survive. Still, "recognizing that there are many things we can learn from other traditions is not the same as insisting that all stories are equally valid."[9]

4. Taking advantage of a noticeable trend toward increasing religious loyalty among that segment of the population that identifies with New Age issues and concerns. "They have the energy and the motivation to become positive contributors."[10]

5. Responding effectively to the fact that among those who are brand-new to any faith tradition at all there is a slight preference for the Presbyterian and Reformed tradition, and an even more remarkable preference for the New Age, for Unitarian-Universalism, and for Eastern religions.

6. Responding constructively to the fact that among those switching from one denominational affiliation to another and whose religious interests are on the rise, there is a search for (1) spiritual teaching, (2) life purpose and direction, and (3) a good church "where something is happening." This group is more racially and ethnically diverse, well-educated and affluent.

7. Parting with past ways that are no longer relevant and effective, relinquishing a past of institutional privilege and cultural establishment for mainline churches, adopting instead a prophetic role over against the false values of contemporary society and culture.

8. Confronting the blockers and obstructionists in the congregation, helping them to grieve their loss of a comfortable and familiar past, affirming their past contributions while challenging them to let go and to let the church move on into a new future.

9. Understanding that the church exists not just for those inside, but also for those outside, particularly those in our own local communities who are most in need of what the gospel has to offer.

10. Understanding that we must *confront the degree to which we have enculturated the gospel and our traditions,* accepting the fact that the two are not the same, and then engaging in the hard work of sorting out the one from the other.[11]

Claiming our Identity

In the above data and in the conclusions Regele draws from them is some measure of hope for the future of progressive mainline churches, but only if we can begin to recover our essential identity, our vision, and our sense of mission. We need to be clear about our core convictions, commitments, and callings so that we can live out our faith and share it with clarity, vigor, and enthusiasm. Many conservative Christians and churches are convinced that they have a life-or-death biblical commission to save souls from eternal damnation. This fuels their mission and evangelism. Is there anything for which we progressives can mount a comparable measure of commitment, passion, and zeal—anything that is of life-or-death significance for us? Let's see if we can answer that question by identifying the kind of church we will have to be.

Being a Gospel Church That Embodies and Shares the Good News

The love of God has been supremely incarnated in Jesus of Nazareth whom we confess to be Lord and Christ, the holistic embodiment in one life of God's redeeming love and delivering power for all people. As his disciples and as his living, mystical body we are called into that divine life and commissioned to continue proclaiming and embodying the good news of God's redeeming love. This is our great commission. We are called and baptized, just as he was, to a risk-taking ministry that is empowered by the Spirit to overcome all the boundaries and barriers between people, to reach out to include within God's loving embrace and ours the least, the last, the lost, the lonely.

We are called and anointed in the power of the Holy Spirit, just as Christ was, to proclaim and to practice divine deliverance for all who are enslaved, imprisoned, exploited, and oppressed. This means confronting and overcoming evil spirits and evil systems, principalities and powers of many and various sorts: unjust and oppressive political and economic systems, the addictive power of drugs and alcohol, a sex- and violence-purveying entertainment industry, the meaninglessness of a life without higher purposes, materialism, racism, sexism, repressive fundamentalisms, and so on.

Being a Whole Gospel Church

It's too bad that the tag "Full Gospel Church" is already taken, but perhaps "Whole Gospel Church" will communicate the vision even better. Jesus called us to love and serve God holistically, with all our heart, mind, soul, and strength, and our neighbors as ourselves. We are called to a faith that integrates the life of the mind, of the emotions, of the soul, of the body, of all our will and energy as we become centered in a loving relationship with that divine One-in-Three who is the source and destination of all being. A Whole Gospel Church is a both/and church, a church that makes no false distinctions between individual salvation and the social gospel, no false distinctions between evangelism and social action, no false distinctions between spirituality and social justice, no false distinctions between a faith for the head and a faith for the heart. The

Whole Gospel vision calls us to a faith that gives equal weight to our intellectual understanding of God, to our personal, spiritual experience of God, and to our energetic action to shape that peaceful, compassionate, and just society toward which Jesus was always pointing—that realm of shalom, of comprehensive well-being, where God's will is done on earth as it is in heaven.

Also essential to our identity and mission as Whole Gospel churches is our ability to be a broad church of open hearts and open minds. We are the ones who can offer spiritual seekers a safe and accepting environment where their questions and concerns will be heard, taken seriously, and imaginatively related to the historic Christian faith within a faith community where no one is expected to think and believe exactly like anyone else. Whole Gospel churches have a calling to carve out and defend a theological middle ground that is neither absolutistic nor relativistic. We have a calling to provide a faith community in which the scriptures are taken seriously but not literally, where the focus is on the big picture in the Bible, not the jots and tittles that can turn the Bible into a repressive, legalistic, moral code book that is used to reject, exclude, and oppress whole groups of people as unacceptable to God.

Being a Universal Gospel Church

There is much in the preceding paragraphs that points us to issues and concerns that are truly of life-and-death significance, that call us to be passionate, committed, zealous agents of God's redeeming love revealed in Jesus Christ. One more life-and-death concern for the whole human family—both now and until the realm of God fully comes—is the spiritual and moral imperative to discover and develop ways we can live together on our one small planet in peace and harmony. Otherwise we can expect many more Bosnias and Kosovos and Rwandas. Otherwise the misguided prejudices and passions of various sorts of sectarianism and fundamentalism will have us constantly at one another's throats.

This universal faith perspective points us to a mission for which progressive mainline Christians, with open minds and open hearts, are especially well equipped. This is a mission that calls us to promote conversation, mutual respect and understanding, and cooperative action across all barriers of race and creed, ethnicity and nationality, sexual identity and gender. It is our mission to explore and to affirm our rich human diversity, even our faith diversity, as a gift from God, not as a cause to reject and destroy one another. It is a mission to discover and to affirm those spiritual, moral treasures we hold in common that can give life-affirming guidance and direction to all God's children everywhere.

Naming the Spiritual Challenges

Beginning with the Introduction and throughout this book we have identified the spiritual challenges involved—both for individual believers and for their congregations—if we are, in the midst of rapid social and cultural change, to change and grow rather than to wither and die. Here, in conclusion, is the place to draw these threads together, to be as clear as we can about the faith-based nature of all the issues and concerns with which we have been grappling. We are dealing here with far more than timely tips and how-to advice for institutional survival. It is, rather, the question of how open we are to let the Holy Spirit transform us and our churches so that we can be God's faithful and fruitful agents of spiritual transformation, engaged in the ministry and mission to which Christ is calling us in our rapidly changing world. Here are the spiritual challenges, most of which we have already named:

1. Responding to the call of Christ as a call to a faith journey, to a life of ongoing transformation, of continuous learning and growing, of repeated conversions, of daily death and resurrection. Nurturing the development of a maturing faith will point us toward the emerging globalism that Regele highlights, toward the universal faith perspective that James Fowler identifies as the most complete development of faith in his influential work *Stages of Faith*.

2. Heeding the promise and warning of the parable of the talents. The gospel of Christ is entrusted to his disciples as a precious spiritual gift that we cannot clutch to ourselves alone within the walls of our comfortable churches. It is a gift that by its very nature must be invested for growth, shared and risked so that others—especially those outside our own cultural comfort zones—may also claim and share the gift of God's love.

3. Seeking from God a degree of spiritual transcendence that will enable us, as much as humanly possible, to stand outside and above ourselves: our class, our culture, our race or ethnicity, our nationalism, our denominationalism, our sexual identity. Only so can we begin to distinguish between the various, unessential cultural accretions to our faith on the one hand, and then, on the other hand, claim the essential core of our faith.

4. Praying for the ability within our progressive and liberal churches to give more than lip service to what we preach about God's concern for those left out and marginalized by our society. Again, this will require facing up to our own classism. It will mean accepting the challenges of change that we ourselves must make within our socially, culturally, racially homogeneous congregations if we are to reach out to and draw into our faith communities those of other classes, races, cultures, and sexual identities about whose plight we claim to care. It will mean, for example, stretching ourselves to learn from, to be enriched and renewed by the spirituality and worship styles of the dispossessed.

5. Seeking from God the courage and the openness to drink from strange wells on our faith journey, taking the risk of appreciating and learning from other cultures, other faith traditions, younger generations, even from those in our own denominations with whom we may have some major theological differences.

6. Encouraging the blockers and obstructionists in our churches to face up to and accept their own spiritual challenge to let go of power and control, to release their death grip on our churches so that God may, indeed, do a new thing in our midst. (Many congregations will probably need the help of outside resources to do this, help, we might hope, that could be provided by their denomination.)

7. Finding ways in our congregations to extend a wide-open welcome to all sorts of seekers, lowering all the unnecessary barriers that keep them from entering our faith communities. Ours is an age of great spiritual hunger, souls thirsting for the living God. Open, caring, nonjudgmental faith communities that are ready and willing to support people in their spiritual journeys will find a great harvest of grateful, responsive seekers.

8. Encouraging and guiding those members and friends who are ready to grow into deeper levels of conviction and commitment. Only so will we nurture the passion and the zeal we need to fuel our mission to the world, convinced that we are bearers of a message with life-or-death consequences for the future of all the earth.

9. Nurturing the development of a holistic life of faith that integrates a personal encounter with the living God, an intellectual grasp of Christian faith, and an engagement in social service and action that serves the biblical vision of a just, compassionate, and peaceful world.

Can we do it? Will we do it? Daryl Conner writes that resilience can be summarized in one word: *hope*. But realistic hope, Conner says, can be developed only as we endure, survive, and learn from the dashing of all our false and easy optimism. Surely we have had enough failures over the past forty years to temper our hope. The question is, Can we begin now to learn from our failures and change our ways? If so, we might be entitled to the measure of hope that Conner holds out: "By approaching change in a disciplined manner, we can become architects of our future. Increasing our resilience will enable us to release our creative energy to invent new possibilities, which would previously have been unthinkable!"[12]

In chapter 1 we focused on *metanoia*, repentance, conversion, as the key to any hope of transforming ourselves and our churches—indeed, as key to the whole Christian spiritual path. Peter Senge, somewhat astonishingly, begins his book on learning organizations by calling attention to this same concept, which as he points out, may quite literally mean a self-transcending mind, capable of changing, learning, and growing. "To grasp the meaning of '*metanoia*' is to grasp the deep meaning of 'learning,' for learning also involves a fundamental shift or movement of mind."[13]

Where do we get our resilience, our hope, our capacity for self-transcendence, our ability to change and learn and grow? These are all gifts of the Holy Spirit, the Third Person of the Holy Trinity whom our mainline churches have for too long now either forgotten or ignored. Jesus said to a puzzled Nicodemus, a leader of the Pharisees who failed to understand Jesus when he spoke of the possibility of being born anew by the power of the Holy Spirit, "Are you a teacher of Israel, and yet you do not understand these things?" (John 3:10).

Finally, these words from the late Henri Nouwen: "The movement of God's Spirit is very gentle, very soft. . . . But that movement is also very persistent, strong, and deep. It changes our hearts radically."[14] Therein lies our hope to change and grow rather than to wither and die, opening ourselves to the power of the Holy Spirit to change our hearts . . . radically.

Afterword: Retrospective and Prospective

Lessons Learned the Hard Way

What have we learned from these ten-plus years at East Liberty Presbyterian Church? In large part, of course, that's what this book has been about. Perhaps the question is, What would you do differently? As I have made clear already, I believe the conflict we struggled through was unavoidable. Plenty of congregational case studies and change theories confirm that. It was like lancing a boil. It brought to the surface some nasty stuff that had to be let out before there could be any healing or closure.

To the extent that our struggles were over turf and power and gatekeeping, there was no way around them. There is plenty of evidence that those who opposed our new directions would have done so regardless, whatever may have been, as the therapists say, "the presenting issues." We would have fought over small things (and in various instances did anyway) if we hadn't had big things to fight over. So, if you have to fight, why not set the terms of the engagement and make it over things that really matter in the long run?

Perhaps we could have made a better effort to get our old-turf people engaged in the strategic planning process. Maybe then we would have had more "buy in" once the plan was officially approved by session. But I doubt it. There were plenty of invitations and plenty of opportunities for everyone who chose to do so to participate in our brainstorming sessions. I think those who chose not to participate opted out because the process was strange, uncomfortable, and threatening for them. In the thick of our conflict, one of our younger aspiring power brokers was asked by a newcomer how decisions were made in the congregation. He replied: "Oh, a few of us get together and work it out." Those with such a mind-set are not accustomed to deciding things in an open-minded, open-ended participatory process such as our congregational planning sessions offered—a setting where no one individual could exercise greater influence than any other, except by the power of a good idea. It is understandably difficult for gatekeepers to participate in a process that disallows any shooting down of others' ideas and assumes that participants will bring to the table only their goodwill and creative thinking.

I certainly learned a hard lesson about the endurance that leadership requires. In 1994–95 I just about lost my ability to persevere, my resiliency, my courage. With hindsight, that may have been because I held unrealistic hopes for our planning process. I counted on it achieving something as close to consensus as we could possibly reach in a diverse congregation, that it would allow us to move forward toward "north" without the dissenters continuing to nip at our heels. That, of course, didn't happen without a fight. In the end, the dissenters may well have miscalculated, thinking their numbers were greater than they were. But, in a sense, that really didn't matter to them. To *their* minds, whatever their numbers might be, they were right and the rest of us were wrong. And that was where *I* miscalculated. I had not taken fully enough into account *their* determination, *their* perseverance. I had also given them advance credit for more goodwill than they displayed. When push came to shove, they were not willing, as I had hoped, graciously to concede to the will of the majority, letting the rest of us move on with our vision.

My family probably has it right that I am sometimes too optimistic about people, too ready to give the benefit of the doubt to those about whom I ought to be more wary, too ready to take the facade of goodwill for the real thing. Looking back now, I would have done better to give more credence to the early warnings I was given about certain groups and certain individuals. As one steeped in the discipline of sociology, I can surely be faulted for taking so long to perceive the informal power and influence of certain congregational sub-cultures, especially for failing to reckon with their ability to "indoctrinate" new-comers in their viewpoints.

In the same connection, I probably ought to have been more political than I was at times. In my role as the staff person on the nominating committee, I could probably have exercised more of an interventionist role than I often did. Not that I refrained from speaking up when names of those who were clearly, chronically oppositional were proposed. There were instances, however, when names were advanced of individuals who were openly on the opposite side of issues on which I thought the church should take a particular stand. I did not speak in opposition to those individuals if they seemed to be persons of good-will and a cooperative spirit. In some of these cases my judgment turned out to be good, in others not so good.

Still, I am not ready to give up on my belief that it is possible for people of goodwill who hold sharply differing views to work together in harmony. I agree with the Rev. Jim Mead, who is our new Pittsburgh Presbytery executive (or "Pastor to Presbytery," as he prefers to be called) and a moderate evangelical, that we should aim to be "a big tent church." Relying on the fruit of the Spirit (Gal. 5:22–23) and a good measure of reasonableness, I still believe that liberal/progressives and evangelical/conservatives (we sketched out some of the characteristics of these two perspectives in chapter 19) should be able to live and work together in the same congregations and the same denominations, agreeing to disagree agreeably. As this book makes clear, I believe that we have important things to learn from one another and that we ought to strive, if at all possible, to remain in dialogue. Realistically, however, we must also accept the fact that, for whatever the reasons, there are certain individuals and groups who would simply rather fight.

Our Accomplishments in Perspective

Our Cathedral of Hope has broken some new ground for a mainline congregation. We have taken risks and tried new things, some of which have worked and some of which have not. In Pittsburgh, "the city of bridges," we have been spiritual bridge builders. We have become an increasingly diverse and inclusive congregation. We have made significant progress in becoming interracial and multicultural. Our socioeconomic class diversity is especially impressive for a Presbyterian church, indeed for any mainline church.

With regard to our social and racial diversity and inclusivity, I must make something of a confession. I know I would not be where I now am in comprehending these challenges if God had not blessed me over the past decade-plus with this calling that has exposed me to so many marvelous opportunities to learn and grow on the frontiers of urban church ministry. I am profoundly grateful and deeply humbled that I was the one called to this high and holy work in this time and place. Yes, I *was* comfortable in my white, suburban, prosperous, stable, upper-middle-class congregation in Evanston. We were located there less than a mile from a predominantly African American neighborhood, on the other side of a drainage canal. We made a few efforts to reach out across that canal, but nothing all that serious, sustained, or effective. I had the ideal then. I knew where I stood but not how to move forward. I didn't know how to build bridges across that canal.

Without the challenging circumstances and experiences of the past ten years, as "afflicting" and painful as some of them have been, I could not have begun to comprehend what it might mean to try to stand outside my own "skin," the skin of my elite education, my racial and social class conditioning. Never would I have wrestled, just to cite one small example, with how on earth one might go about offering new member orientation and instruction to groups that often include both Ph.D.'s as well as some who lack basic literacy skills. And how about preaching to such a diverse congregation? Talk about a learning environment for the teacher!

In terms of our numerical growth, we must also be somewhat humble. In fact, our official membership is actually less than it was ten years ago. That is partly because we have been conscientious about "cleaning" our membership rolls annually to remove inactives. It also is because quite a number of new people have affiliated as "friends of the church" rather than as members and thus do not show up on our official rolls. In any case, students of church growth know that church membership figures are notoriously unreliable and that the far more significant numbers are those of average worship attendance. On that score, our record looks much better. Worship attendance has doubled in the past ten years, no little feat for a congregation in an inner-city neighborhood that has a reputation (somewhat undeserved) for being unsafe. Still, that hardly qualifies as significant in comparison to the fantastic growth rates of many megachurches and new paradigm churches, though most of them are not aiming simultaneously to become interracial, multicultural faith communities.

The terrific impediment to church growth that our neighborhood's image problem constitutes for us is illustrated by a conversation my wife and I had about five years ago with a young interior decorator at a suburban furniture store. White, in her twenties, she expressed delight when she learned who we were. "Oh," she exclaimed, "my fiancé and I love your church! We worshiped there last summer and we said to each other, 'This is it! This is where we want to be married, and this is where we want to make our church home.' However," she continued, "when we told our parents, my future in-laws said, 'No way! We will not have this wedding in East Liberty!' So," she concluded sadly, "we have had to find a suburban Presbyterian church."

As far as financial risk taking is concerned, I know that we cannot hold a candle to many other congregations who take great leaps of faith to borrow large sums of money to build new facilities and undertake new ministries. The neocharismatic new paradigm churches are especially impressive in this regard. Their ministers take considerable risk with their careers and their personal finance when they launch risky new church start-ups with no guarantee of any initial income whatsoever. I know several local examples of pastors and non-denominational, multiracial congregations that have displayed similar faith and courage.

Yes, at East Liberty we have regularly budgeted expenditures from our endowment at percentages considerably in excess of what is typically considered prudent for not-for-profit organizations—consistent with the "grow the church," "prudent risk-taking" policy set forth in our 1994 strategic plan. Still, our total endowment value has grown from $18 million in 1988 to $37 million in late-1999! So, as far as setting any monetary risk-taking standards is concerned, we still have a long way to go.

More Work to Be Done

In the fall of 1998 we started a second round of strategic planning. The new committee has carefully reviewed the 1994 plan and come to agreement that it is still, as far as our major program goals are concerned, a very sound plan. In fact, an architect we recently hired as a facilities and community development planning consultant has told us that in her extensive work with a wide array of not-for-profit organizations, it is the best and most complete plan of its kind that she has ever seen!

In early 1999 we brought on board for a short stint a consultant to work with our planning committee, Carolyn Weese, director of Multi-Staff Ministries, based in Phoenix, and author of *Eagles in Tall Steeples*.[1] In addition to making some sensible recommendations for redesigning our office support team, Carolyn also helped us to design a congregational survey and a series of focus groups on various major planning topics. All our members and friends were invited to participate. Both the survey results and the focus groups confirmed the planning committee's judgment that basically we still have a good plan and should continue working it. The survey and the focus groups did, however, help us to identify certain areas of priority concern for the congregation, areas where we need to put more emphasis and work harder: (1) youth and young adult ministry, (2) better training and integration into church life for new members, (3) parking and security concerns, (4) stewardship, and (5) community development.

None of this came as a surprise to our new planning committee, to our lay leaders, or to our ministry and program staff. Our session decided a year ago, for example, to replace our three part-time youth workers with one full-time ordained minister for youth and young adults. It is significant that we agreed that the person chosen for that position need not be a Presbyterian. Because we were especially concerned to find the best person and to give full consideration to African American candidates, we conducted a two-track search: one within the Presbyterian system and a second in the "open market." Our candidate, chosen in late 1999, is an African American, United Church of Christ minister with years of successful experience working with diverse groups of youth, both black and white, urban and suburban.

Carolyn also encouraged and inspired us to focus on parking, security, and community development as top priority concerns. She told us that in her opinion our congregation was not likely to experience any further significant growth unless we could effectively address our community image and related safety and security perceptions. We must do something to acquire space for a well-lighted and security-attended church parking lot adjacent to the church building. We also need to consider how the church can further contribute to the improvement of the commercial area that surrounds the church on all four sides. In that regard, as previously mentioned in chapter 17, one of the community improvement projects we are currently pursuing is the reopening of the community theater directly across the street from the front of the church. In addition, we are presently discussing the possibility of acquiring property adjacent to the church to develop as a community youth center. For these reasons we have retained a facilities and community development consultant to help us study and assess all these possibilities.

Carolyn Weese has had fifteen years of experience consulting with large churches coast to coast, primarily with conservative evangelical churches, many of them Presbyterian churches. I first met her at a church growth conference held at a conservative evangelical Presbyterian church in Texas. When I inquired about the possibility of her assisting us in Pittsburgh, I was careful to explain that East Liberty Presbyterian Church was probably a more liberal church than those with which she was accustomed to working. She assured me, nevertheless, that she would be both comfortable and eager to work with us. Later, after she had spent several intensive days with us, interviewing staff and lay leaders, sitting in on committee meetings and worship services, Carolyn said to our session: "When Dr. Chesnut first told me that you were a liberal church, I was fully expecting to come here and find that God was dead! However," she continued, "as soon as I set foot in your building, I felt the

Spirit's presence. In fact," she concluded, "in all my years of church consulting, I don't believe that I have encountered another congregation more deeply spiritual than yours." That heartening assessment leads us now into consideration of another new direction for future ministry priorities at East Liberty—going deeper with our faith.

Moving toward the Deep End

I have long spoken of the church as being somewhat like a swimming pool—a public pool, of course, not a country club pool. Like a swimming pool, we offer a deep end and a shallow end. We say to people, "Come on in, the water's fine. Get in where you're comfortable. If you want to sit on the edge of the pool and dangle your toes in the water to start with, that's fine. If you want to wade around in the shallow end for a while, go ahead. We do, however, also have a deep end, a high diving board, instructors and trained people to help you when you feel ready to move in that direction."

The problem with our mainline churches, however, may be that we often don't do such a good job of encouraging and enabling people to move to the deeper end. We go broad rather than deep. Certainly that's true for us at East Liberty. We are responding well to people's deep spiritual hunger, but we are also recognizing that we need to do a much better job of discipling our people, helping them to grow in their faith and in their Christian commitment. One step our ministry and program staff is taking in that direction is to begin offering a basic adult education series that will provide an introduction to Christian faith and life, a variety of courses that will be repeated each year. It will encompass individual segments providing introductions to the Bible, to Christian doctrine, to the spiritual disciplines and gifts, and to Christian ethics and social concerns. We are calling it "Seeds": Search, Enlighten, Enthuse, Deepen, Serve.

In addition, our staff has also begun exploring how we might offer a variety of paths of discipline that would provide encouragement and guidance for our members and friends as a way to deepen their faith commitments. This would probably be over and above the basic commitments made when people join the church. One path might be related to the Taizé community. One path might be modeled on the pattern developed at the well-known Church of the Saviour in Washington, D.C. It would include commitments to Christian study, to stewardship, to spiritual disciplines, to social service and action. Another path might tie in with the disciplines involved in affiliation with the worldwide fellowship of the Iona Community in Scotland. Another path might be especially designed for seekers who are not yet ready to make explicitly Christian faith commitments, but who do want to formalize their intentions to pursue a disciplined spiritual journey in company with kindred spirits. One way in which this overall pattern might be conceived is something akin to a variety of lay orders, somewhat comparable to the variety of religious orders and their lay affiliates offered in the Roman Catholic Church.

One very interesting implication that such thinking and such possibilities spark in my own imagination is the thought that our larger mainline congregations might aspire to being truly whole, truly "catholic" churches by offering within one and the same community of faith alternative patterns and paths of affiliation and commitment. If these alternative paths were to correspond to those three major, social and historical types explored by Ernst Troeltsch a century ago (see chapter 18), they might take shape something like this: (1) *the church type*, which is broad and inclusive, welcoming all comers, giving people who want it plenty of space and opportunity for open-ended exploration, allowing people freedom to move at their own pace; (2) *the sect type*, which is much more voluntarily rigorous, disciplined, and committed in its focus on the Christian faith and the disciplines of the Christian life; (3) *the mystical type*, which welcomes the seekers, the broader and freer thinkers who are nevertheless quite serious about the spiritual life and very possibly eager to make greater personal and communal commitments within a company of fellow pilgrims and kindred spirits who are more focused on spiritual growth than on institutional maintenance and organizational routines.

I think this concept may hold considerable promise as a creative and faithful way by which mainline churches can move in the direction of nurturing deeper commitment while simultaneously honoring different individual paths. This would be responsive to one of the new millennium challenges highlighted by Cimino and Lattin, namely, to encourage those in our churches who feel a need for deeper spiritual experience and commitment without making either these "spiritual virtuosi" or our more nominal members feel uncomfortable together within the same congregation. Once again, however, this will obviously require continuing efforts to nurture within and among ourselves a deep mutual respect and appreciation that will allow us to honor and celebrate a wide and rich diversity of individual spiritual journeys. I think we should take heart because this celebration of diversity is a Christian virtue that ought to be highly valued in our progressive mainline congregations.

Moving toward North

Goethe wrote, "I have come to see that the main thing is not where we stand, but in what direction we are moving." For some time now, most of our mainline churches have claimed to stand for racial and social justice, equality, diversity, and inclusiveness. But is that the direction in which we are moving? Liberal or progressive mainliners long ago rightly rejected as theologically and ethically deficient the evangelical church growth movement's "homogeneous unit" concept—the notion that to grow a church successfully requires that the people be racially and socially homogeneous. In actuality, however, are not most of our liberal or progressive congregations also homogeneous units? And are we doing anything really serious to rectify this situation? Not on any significant

scale as far as I can see. Our Presbyterian congregations are even more racially
ethnically segregated than the overall denominational statistics indicate. Yes, 7
percent of Presbyterian Church (U.S.A.) members nationwide are racial ethnic
members, but most of these are not to be found in racially mixed congregations,
but rather in congregations that are themselves homogeneously African
American or Asian American in composition.

While our society as a whole seems more and more willing to affirm ideals
of diversity and inclusivity, we are in some respects becoming a more racially,
ethnically, and socially segregated nation. The growth of suburban sprawl continues unabated in the United States[2] as the geographical divides between rich
and poor, between whites and minorities become wider and wider. While it is
true that an increasing percentage of our minorities are now residing in suburban communities, most of these individuals are likely to be living still in highly segregated communities—the only difference being that it is now *suburban*
segregation.

With the increasing abandonment of busing as a strategy for achieving racial
and social integration and equality of educational opportunity within the public
schools, our schools themselves are becoming resegregated. Orlando Patterson,
professor of sociology at Harvard University, has recently cited the disturbing
statistics, calling this "the nation's single greatest failure in its generally successful effort to right the wrongs of its racist past: our inability to integrate our
schools and our communities."[3] Of course, the reason we cannot integrate our
neighborhood schools, as Patterson reminds us, is that we have not integrated
our neighborhoods. Furthermore, he maintains, America is also becoming more
and more residentially segregated by class, a segregation that cuts across race
lines and results in isolating those of lower class—whites, blacks, Hispanics
alike—from exposure to dominant cultural norms.

With understandable frustration, Patterson calls our attention to the solid
research evidence that whites who went to integrated schools or grew up in
mixed neighborhoods are more likely to have a positive view of diversity. So
what to do? Busing is a lost cause and most people do not support any sort of
governmentally imposed solutions to these national, social and ethical dilemmas. Here is his conclusion:

> Busing is dead, but let us seize the opportunity to do the right thing by
> working toward the integration of our neighborhoods. By doing so, we
> will not only solve the educational problems of our minorities and
> greatly enhance their network and cultural resources, but also make for
> a more tolerant and genuinely multiethnic nation.[4]

Close to forty years ago now, as we pointed out in the Introduction, Gibson
Winter struggled with these same dilemmas in his challenge to the churches
entitled *The Suburban Captivity of the Churches*. He forthrightly named there

"the peculiar dilemma confronting Protestantism in the metropolis: How can an inclusive message be mediated through an exclusive group, when the principle of exclusiveness is social class [and racial] identity rather than a gift of faith which is open to all?" Four decades later and with virtually no progress to show, is it utterly unrealistic to hope that our churches might still be able, even at this late date, to make some positive contribution here? Might God possibly give us a second chance to lead the way in constructively addressing this social and ethical dilemma that lies so close to the heart of our professed ideals as Christians and as Americans? What institution besides the church has the moral and spiritual standing to so influence our local communities? As this book has maintained from start to finish, mainline churches could start by making truly conscientious efforts to transform our own congregations, in accord with our professed ideals, into more truly diverse and inclusive faith communities.

What began four decades ago as the Blake-Pike proposal for mainline Protestant church union may finally now be offering us a glimmer of hope and the organizational framework for moving toward this vision of greater diversity and inclusivity in church and society. The elusive goal of total organic church union was given up long ago, and the proposal is now called "Churches Uniting in Christ" (CUIC). CUIC offers us a vision of bringing nine historic Protestant denominations, including three large, predominantly African American denominations, together around our Lord's Table, together in mutual recognition of one another's ministries and sacraments, together *in a united Christian effort to overcome racism in America.* If we will start in our local churches and communities, reaching out to one another across denominational, social, and racial barriers, then maybe we can begin learning from one another how to start practicing what we have for so long been preaching only. This is certainly not a new idea, but how many white congregations, for example, are effectively linked with another congregation of a different racial ethnic composition, exchanging pulpits and choirs and even members as well as engaging in mission together? What better way to start getting outside our own "skins," learning not only to accept but to celebrate the culturally and spiritually rich gifts of faith and praise that our diverse traditions have to offer one another?

It is my hope and prayer that this book will make a constructive contribution in moving others toward the realization of this vision. I do believe that our Pittsburgh bridge-building designs and skills are exportable. So, may our Cathedral of Hope innovations and experiments, our dreams and our visions, our successes and our failures offer hope to you, to your church, and to the larger church: hope, inspiration, practical guidance, and a vision of new possibilities.

If we recommit ourselves to God's larger vision for us and pray for God's guidance in moving us toward something greater and grander than simply our own institutional survival, then we may hope anew. We may hope to become churches that deserve not only to survive but also to thrive. We may hope to experience the rebirth in a new millennium of that amazingly diverse and inclusive Church of Jesus Christ first given birth at Pentecost—a church that is, by the power of the Holy Spirit, both transformed and transforming.

For more information about the Cathedral of Hope, visit our Web site at www.cathedralofhope.org. Also, for a copy of our church video, *Welcome to the Cathedral of Hope*, please send $8.00 to East Liberty Presbyterian Church, 116 S. Highland Ave., Pittsburgh, PA 15206.

APPENDIX

———◆———

Creative Advertising

Handel's *Messiah*, Holy Week Portions, March 24, 11 AM
Penn and Highland Avenues • Pittsburgh, PA 15206 • 441-3800

"**I**t's a 200 year old church that understands 23 year olds."

"A lot of people think students just party all the time. That we don't understand real issues.

This church is different. They share my uncertainty about careers, my life and the world. These people reached out and made me a part of this church."

East Liberty Presbyterian Church

Handel's *Messiah*, Holy Week Portions, March 24, 11 AM
Penn and Highland Avenues • Pittsburgh, PA 15206 • 441-3800

"Finally a church that knew I had a mind along with my soul."

"This church will challenge you. One look at their work in East Liberty and you'll know that East Liberty Presbyterian Church isn't ducking the tough questions about drugs, economic justice, poverty and divorce. They're asking them."

East Liberty Presbyterian Church

Penn State Choir & Orchestra, April 21, 11 AM
Penn and Highland Avenues • Pittsburgh, PA 15206 • 441-3800

Notes

Introduction

1. Gibson Winter, *The Suburban Captivity of the Churches: An Analysis of Protestant Responsibility in the Expanding Metropolis* (Garden City, N.Y.: Doubleday & Co., 1961), 29.
2. "Latino America," *Newsweek*, July 12, 1999, 48–51.
3. Samuel G. Freedman, "Suburbia Outgrows Its Image," *New York Times*, Feb. 28, 1999, A & L, sec. 2, p. 1.
4. *Presbyterian News Briefs*, Feb. 5, 1999, 11.
5. *Presbyterian News Briefs,* Oct. 9, 1998, 9.

Chapter 3. Would We Rather Die than Change?

1. John W. Gardner, *Self-Renewal: The Individual and the Innovative Society* (New York: Harper & Row, 1963), 53.

Chapter 5. Drinking from Strange Wells

1. Doug Murren, *The Baby Boomerang: Catching the Baby Boomers as They Come Back to Church* (Ventura, Calif.: Regal Books/Gospel Light, 1990).

Chapter 6. A Pilgrimage of Trust

1. *Songs and Prayers from Taizé* (Chicago: GIA Publications, 1991). All Taizé songs cited herein are from this source.
2. Thomas Moore, *Care of the Soul* (New York: HarperCollins, 1992), 145–48.

Chapter 7. Becoming the Cathedral of Hope

1. Nancy T. Ammerman, *Congregation and Community* (New Brunswick, N.J.: Rutgers University Press, 1997), 327.

Chapter 8. Reaching a Generation of Seekers

1. Wade Clark Roof, *A Generation of Seekers: The Spiritual Journeys of the Baby Boom Generation* (San Francisco: Harper, 1993), 8.
2. Ibid., 26.
3. Matthew Fox, *Original Blessing* (Santa Fe, N.Mex.: Bear & Co., 1983); *The Coming of the Cosmic Christ* (San Francisco: Harper, 1988).
4. Matthew Fox, *Creation Spirituality: Liberating Gifts for the Peoples of the Earth* (San Francisco: Harper, 1991).
5. Duncan S. Ferguson, ed., *New Age Spirituality: An Assessment* (Louisville, Ky.: Westminster/John Knox Press, 1993).
6. Wade Clark Roof, *Christian Century,* March 19, 1999, 318–19.

7. James Redfield, *The Celestine Prophecy* (New York: Warner Books, 1993); Jaroslav Pelikan, *Jesus through the Centuries: His Place in the History of Culture* (New York: Harper & Row, 1985); Howard L. Rice, *Reformed Spirituality* (Louisville, Ky.: Westminster/John Knox Press, 1991); Michael Lerner, *The Politics of Meaning: Restoring Hope in an Age of Cynicism* (Reading, Mass.: Addison-Wesley Publishing Co., 1996); Thomas Moore, *Care of the Soul* (New York: Harper Collins, 1992); Huston Smith, *The Illustrated World's Religions: A Guide to Our Wisdom Traditions* (San Francisco: Harper, 1994); Elizabeth A. Johnson, *She Who Is: The Mystery of God in Feminist Theological Discourse* (New York: Crossroad, 1992); Thich Nhat Hanh, *Living Buddha, Living Christ* (New York: Riverhead Books, 1995).

Chapter 9. A Tale of Two Churches

1. George D. Exoo, "The Cathedral of Hope," *Presbyerian Survey*, October 1994, 20–24.
2. Ammerman, *Congregation and Community*, 335.
3. Ibid., 334.
4. M. Scott Peck, *People of the Lie* (New York: Simon & Schuster, 1983), 76–77.
5. G. Lloyd Rediger, *Clergy Killers: Guidance for Pastors and Congregations under Attack* (Louisville, Ky.: Westminster John Knox Press, 1997).
6. Peter L. Steinke, *Healthy Congregations: A Systems Approach* (Washington, D.C.: Alban Institute, 1996).
7. Peter L. Steinke, "When Congregations Are Stuck," *Christian Century*, April 7, 1999, 387.
8. Stephen Covey, *The Seven Habits of Highly Effective People: Restoring the Character Ethic* (New York: Simon & Schuster, 1989).

Chapter 11. Facing the Music

1. Moore, *Care of the Soul*, 58–59.
2. Ibid., 283.
3. Ibid., 290–91.

Chapter 13. *Annus Horribilis*

1. Hugh F. Halverstadt, *Managing Church Conflict* (Louisville, Ky.: Westminster/John Knox Press, 1991).

Chapter 14. Putting Humpty-Dumpty Together Again

1. Chuck Olsen, *Transforming Church Boards into Communities of Spiritual Leaders* (Washington, D.C.: Alban Institute, 1995).
2. *Is Christ Divided? A Report Approved by the 200th General Assembly (1988) of the Presbyterian Church (U.S.A.)* (Louisville, Ky.: Office of the General Assembly, Presbyterian Church (U.S.A.), 1988), 45 (emphasis added).
3. *Presbyterian Understanding and Use of Holy Scripture* and *Biblical Authority and Interpretation* (Louisville, Ky.: Office of the General Assembly, Presbyterian Church (U.S.A.), 1992).

Chapter 15. Back to the Vision

1. Lauren Artress, *Walking a Sacred Path: Rediscovering the Labyrinth as a Spiritual Tool* (New York: Riverhead Books, 1995).

Chapter 16. Basement Treasure I: Bloom Where You're Planted

1. R. Andrew Chesnut, *Born Again in Brazil: The Pentecostal Boom and the Pathogens of Poverty* (New Brunswick, N.J.: Rutgers University Press, 1997).
2. Alfred, Lord Tennyson, *The Higher Pantheism,* stanza 6.

Chapter 17. Basement Treasure II: Mission at Our Doorstep

1. Mel White, *Stranger at the Gate: To Be Gay and Christian in America* (New York: Penguin Books, 1995).

Chapter 18. Learning from the Trends: Past, Present, and Future

1. Ernst Troeltsch, *The Social Teaching of the Christian Churches*, vols. 1 and 2 (Louisville, Ky.: Westminster/John Knox Press, 1992).
2. Peter Taylor Forsyth, *The Work of Christ* (1910; London: Independent Press, 1938), xxxi.
3. Donald E. Miller, *Reinventing American Protestantism: Christianity in the New Millennium* (Berkeley: University of California Press, 1997).
4. Richard Cimino and Don Lattin, *Shopping for Faith: American Religion in the New Millennium* (San Francisco: Jossey-Bass, 1998).
5. Wade Clark Roof, *Christian Century,* March 19, 1999, 318–19.
6. Cimino and Lattin, *Shopping for Faith,* 189.

Chapter 19. Evaluating the Trends

1. Shirley C. Guthrie, *Christian Doctrine,* rev. ed. (Louisville, Ky.: Westminster John Knox Press, 1994).
2. *Christian Believer: Knowing God with Heart and Mind* (Nashville: Abingdon Press, 1999).
3. Robert McAfee Brown, *Spirituality and Liberation* (Louisville, Ky.: Westminster/John Knox Press, 1988).
4. Susan Hale, *Sound and Silence: Voicing the Soul* (Albuquerque, N.Mex.: La Alameda Press, 1995).
5. Gustaf Aulén, *Christus Victor: An Historical Study of the Three Main Types of the Idea of Atonement* (New York: Macmillan Co., 1951).

Chapter 20. Transforming People, Transforming Organizations

1. Warren Bennis, *Leaders: The Strategies for Taking Charge* (New York: Harper & Row, 1985).
2. Daryl Conner, *Managing at the Speed of Change* (New York: Villard Books, 1992).
3. Harry S. Dent Jr., *The Roaring 2000s* (New York: Simon & Schuster, 1998), 54.
4. Ibid., 13–14.
5. Peter Senge, *The Fifth Discipline: The Art and Practice of the Learning Organization* (New York: Doubleday & Co., 1990), 34.

6. Dent, *Roaring 2000s,* 200.
7. Mike Regele, with Mark Schulz, *The Death of the Church* (Grand Rapids: Zondervan Publishing House, 1995).
8. James W. Fowler, *Stages of Faith: The Psychology of Human Development and the Quest for Meaning* (San Francisco: Harper & Row, 1981).
9. Dent, *Roaring 2000s,* 172.
10. Senge, *Fifth Discipline,* 341.
11. Dent, *Roaring 2000s,* 136.
12. Ibid., 137–38.

Chapter 21. What Is the Hope for Mainline Churches?

1. Roger Finke and Rodney Stark, *The Churching of America, 1776–1990: Winners and Losers in Our Religious Economy* (New Brunswick, N.J.: Rutgers University Press, 1992).
2. Dean M. Kelley, *Why Conservative Churches Are Growing* (New York: Harper & Row, 1972).
3. Regele, *Death of the Church,* 51.
4. Ibid., 108.
5. Ibid., 124.
6. Dent, *Roaring 2000s,* 183.
7. Ibid., 190.
8. Regele, *Death of the Church,* 93.
9. Ibid., 205.
10. Ibid., 150.
11. Ibid., 198.
12. Conner, *Managing at the Speed of Change,* 272–73.
13. Senge, *Fifth Discipline,* 13.
14. Henri Nouwen, *Life of the Beloved: Spiritual Living in a Secular World* (New York: Crossroad, 1997), 63.

Afterword: Retrospective and Prospective

1. Carolyn Weese, *Eagles in Tall Steeples: What Pastors and Congregations Wish They Knew about Each Other* (Nashville: Thomas Nelson Publishers, 1991).
2. "Sprawling, Sprawling," *Newsweek,* July 19, 1999, 23–27.
3. Orlando Patterson, "What to Do When Busing Becomes Irrelevant," *New York Times,* July 18, 1999, Op-Ed, 17.
4. Ibid.